STUDIES IN ECONOMIC AND SOCIAL HISTORY

This series, specially commissioned by the Economic History Society, provides a guide to the current interpretations of the key themes of economic and social history in which advances have recently been made or in which there has been significant debate.

Origally entitled 'Studies in Economic History', in 1974 the series had its scope extended to include topics in social history, and the new series title, 'Studies in Economic and Social History', signalises this development.

The series gives readers access to the best work done, helps them to draw their own conclusions in major fields of study, and by means of the critical bibliography in each book guides them in the selection of further reading. The aim is to provide a spring-board to further work rather than a set of pre-packaged conclusions or short-cuts.

STUDIES IN ECONOMIC AND SOCIAL HISTORY

Edited for the Economic History Society by T. C. Smout

PUBLISHED

OTHER TITLES ARE IN PREPARATION

The American Frontier Revisited

Prepared for
The Economic History Society by
MARGARET WALSH

Lecturer in Economic and Social History,
University of Birmingham

HUMANITIES PRESS
Atlantic Highlands, New Jersey 1981

© The Economic History Society 1981

First published 1981 in the U.S.A. by
HUMANITIES PRESS INC.
Atlantic Highlands, N.J. 07716

Printed in Hong Kong

Library of Congress Cataloging in Publication Data

Walsh, Margaret.
    The American frontier revisited.

    (Studies in economic and social history)
    Bibliography: p.
    Includes index.
        1.   United States—Territorial expansion.   2.   Land
use, Rural—United States.   3.   The West—Economic conditions.   4.   Frontier thesis.   I.   Title.
E179.5.W34   330.978   80-36857
ISBN 0—391—02098—6

Contents

Maps

Tables

Acknowledgements

It would be impossible to acknowledge the full debt owed to numerous friends, colleagues and librarians, on both sides of the Atlantic, who have encouraged me to work and teach in the field of Western history. I am, however, especially grateful to three sets of people. Firstly, Jim Potter and Peter Cain both offered valuable and pertinent criticisms on early versions of the manuscript. Secondly, the Huntington Library generously provided me with a summer fellowship whereby I was privileged to enjoy the resources and companionship of what must rank as a Western scholar's 'El Dorado'. Thirdly, several years of undergraduate students at the University of Birmingham, have, for better or for worse, 'gone west', and in doing so, have provided me with an audience for exploring and testing ideas. I alone am responsible for any errors in the text.

Note on References

References in the text within brackets relate to the entries in the Select Bibliography.

Editor's Preface

SINCE 1968, when the Economic History Society and Macmillan published the first of the 'Studies in Economic and Social History', the series has established itself as a major teaching tool in universities, colleges and schools, and as a familiar landmark in serious bookshops throughout the country. A great deal of the credit for this must go to the wise leadership of its first editor, Professor M. W. Flinn, who retired at the end of 1977. The books tend to be bigger now than they were originally, and inevitably more expensive; but they have continued to provide information in modest compass at a reasonable price by the standards of modern academic publication.

There is no intention of departing from the principles of the first decade. Each book aims to survey findings and discussion in an important field of economic or social history that has been the subject of recent lively debate. It is meant as an introduction for readers who are not themselves professional researchers but who want to know what the discussion is all about – students, teachers and others generally interested in the subject. The authors, rather than either taking a strongly partisan line or suppressing their own critical faculties, set out the arguments and the problems as fairly as they can, and attempt a critical summary and explanation of them from their own judgement. The discipline now embraces so wide a field in the study of the human past that it would be inappropriate for each book to follow an identical plan, but all volumes will normally contain an extensive descriptive bibliography.

The series is not meant to provide all the answers but to help readers to see the problems clearly enough to form their own conclusions. We shall never agree in history, but the discipline will be well served if we know what we are disagreeing about, and why.

T. C. SMOUT

University of St Andrews

Editor

1 The Significance of the Frontier Thesis in American Economic History

IN 1893 a young scholar, Frederick Jackson Turner, presented one of the most celebrated and influential papers in American history, namely 'The Significance of the Frontier in American History'. His thesis contained a set of vital suggestions about American development and provided a viable and unifying framework for understanding the growth of the American West. Though subsequent generations have attacked the thesis, the questions which Turner asked are still the most interesting ones, and it seems unlikely either that any new questions, or a better alternative framework will be forthcoming in the near future.

THE THESIS

The most important proposition in Turner's Frontier thesis is that 'The existence of an area of free land, its continuous recession and the advance of American settlement westward, explain American development' [F. J. Turner, 1893]. The abundance of available and cheap lands, and of a rich resource base, provided opportunities which enabled the United States to grow rapidly through the endeavours of millions of persons. It thus followed that 'The true point of view in the history of the nation is not the Atlantic coast, it is the Great West' [F. J. Turner 1893].

Beginning in the seventeenth century, settlers advanced inland from the Atlantic coastal areas to utilise this wealth. They moved in a repetitive series of evolutionary stages progressing from simple to complex.

'the record . . . begins with the Indian and the hunter . . . it goes on to tell of . . . the entrance of the trader . . . of the pastoral stage in ranch life, the exploitation of the soil by the raising of unrotated crops . . . in sparsely settled communities; the intensive culture of the denser farm settlement; and finally the manufacturing organization with city and factory system' [F. J. Turner, 1893].

It was possible to 'Stand at Cumberland Gap and watch the procession of civilization, marching single file . . . [and] . . . Stand at South Pass in the Rockies a century later and see the same procession with wider intervals between' [F. J. Turner, 1893]. Economic opportunity would be attained through these stages of growth.

But this pattern was drawing to an end in the 1880s, for the frontier as a place was no longer readily visible. Whether defined as

> the outer edge of the wave — the meeting point between savagery and civilization . . . at the further edge of free land . . . (or as) the margin of settlement which has a density of two or more to the square mile . . . (then in either case) . . . The Superintendent of the census for 1890 reports . . . that the settlements of the West lie so scattered over the region that there can no longer be said to be a frontier line [F. J. Turner, 1893].

The disappearance of the frontier 'closed the first period of American history' (F. J. Turner, 1893) and in future Americans would have to seek other sources of opportunity.

The frontier not only shaped American development; it was also the source of American character and identity. The sweep of settlement westwards involved a constant retreat from European influences and a steady growth of independence. Indeed 'the frontier is the line of most rapid and effective Americanization' [F. J. Turner, 1893]. During each move pioneers adjusted to new geographical environments, casting aside their cultural baggage and the complexities of civilised societies. In these frontier encounters they created the new person, the American, who was identified by

> that coarseness and strength combined with acuteness and inquisitiveness; that practical inventive turn of mind, quick to find expendients; that masterful grasp of material things, lacking in the artistic, but powerful to effect great ends; that restless nervous energy, that dominant individualism . . . and withal that buoyance and exuberance which comes with freedom. [F. J. Turner, 1893.]

Frontier traits and American traits were identical because the frontier experience was transmitted as a whole over space and time [H. N. Scheiber, 1969 b].

The outstanding feature of this perennial rebirth was 'the promotion of democracy here and in Europe' [F. J. Turner, 1893]. As settlers adapted to their new surroundings and were forced to participate in public affairs, they gained a broad sense of personal competence and came to regard themselves as equals. Democratic ideas flourished naturally and spread everywhere. 'The frontier States that came into the Union in the first quarter of a century of its existence came in with democratic suffrage provisions and had reactive effects of the highest importance.' [F. J. Turner, 1893]. The pioneer, convinced of democratic participation became the democrat-promoter [S. Elkins and E. McKitrick, 1954].

THE ORIGINS OF THE THESIS

Turner was not the first historian to find the West a source of inspiration, but he was interested in an analytical approach which stressed socio-economic developments rather than a romantic narrative endowed with colourful incidents and folk heroes. He wished to plant the West in the mainstream of historical scholarship. In taking this stance he rejected the current orthodoxy which stressed the importance of the Teutonic origins of American institutions and ideas, and thus the primacy of political history, the Eastern seaboard and the colonial era of American development. Influenced partly by his Midwestern upbringing and education, he recognised the need to pay more attention to place rather than to time and tradition. American history could not be understood without a proper appreciation of the West [L. Benson, 1951; W. R. Jacobs, 1968; R. Hofstadter, 1968; R. A. Billington, 1971, 1973].

Turner also recognised the need to broaden the base for understanding human behaviour. Here he was stimulated by colleagues in other disciplines, and he was convinced that the tools of economists, geographers, sociologists, biologists and statisticians must be used by the historian. In attempting to incorporate the theories and techniques of early social scientists Turner welded Darwin's evolutionary hypothesis on to the physical environment in a type of geographical determinism. The evidence for the analytical basis of his frontier hypothesis was provided by the new field of statistical cartography, which depicted the nation's expansion in graphic format [H. Gannett, 1898; W. R. Jacobs, 1968; R. A. Billington, 1971]. The end-result, however, was not an obtuse piece of scholarship for a specialist audience. Turner wrote a general thesis stated simply within the framework of the historical facts [H. C. Allen, 1957; W. R. Jacobs, 1968; H. R. Lamar, 1969; R. A. Billington, 1971].

He further incorporated an awareness of contemporary events. Clearly his essay reflected the emerging confidence of American nationalism in the 1880s and 1890s by demonstrating its internal — and perhaps even unique — sources of growth. He was also aware of the popular interest in the closing of the public domain, and of the disquiet voiced about the new directions which the nation could take. His talent not only enabled him to adopt new techniques and to synthesise general issues but also to popularise current ideas in clear terms [H. C. Allen, 1957; R. A. Billington, 1971].

The Frontier thesis received little professional recognition at first, partly because it ran counter to traditional interpretations, and partly because its sweeping generalisations did not meet the rigorous standards of scientific analysis. But as Turner spread his ideas widely through his teaching skills and reinforced them in other articles and papers, the 'Significance of the Frontier' became generally accepted as a dynamic interpretation of the American experience. Indeed Turner came to dominate the shape of historical work and had an influence stretching beyond academia in the early decades of the present century. It was not until the Depression years of the 1930s that a group of younger scholars started to attack the Frontier hypothesis on a variety of grounds [G. M. Gressley, 1958; R. A. Billington, 1966; J. K. Putnam, 1976].

There were two main critical thrusts; either the frontier was regarded as an inappropriate interpretative framework for understanding American history, or component parts of the thesis were ambiguous, incompatible or incorrect. Some historians suggested that alternative and better general themes were the class struggle, the economic forces of capitalism, the level of technology, the growth of urbanisation, the immigrant experience or the role of continuity and tradition [D. M. Potter, 1954; H.C. Allen, 1957; G.M. Gressley, 1958; R. A. Billington, 1963]. Other historians commented that the word 'frontier' was used inconsistently and the characteristics associated with pioneer communities were sometimes contradictory and sometimes mutually exclusive. Furthermore Turner's model of development was static and could not readily incorporate change. Specialists argued that the West did not act as a safety-valve for the discontented, land was not free, opportunity was not equal, nor was democracy a frontier product. The list of particular faults was lengthy [G. M. Gressley, 1958; R. A. Billington, 1963; H. N. Scheiber, 1969 b; J. K. Putnam, 1976].

While many criticisms are undeniably valid, Turner's thesis has not been relegated to the historical dustbin. Much of his essay remains viable and suggestive, and the work of another generation of behavioural scientists in the past quarter-century testifies that Turner still stands head and shoulders above any rivals. Certainly he overemphasised environment in his efforts to bypass the Teutonic germ theory and create a distinctive American interpretation. Empirical research has shown that there was no single pattern of development shared by all frontiers. The so-called pioneer characteristics can be found in older-established areas and indeed causal lines might run east to west rather than vice versa. Opportunity on the frontier was not necessarily better than elsewhere and it is very difficult to demonstrate how frontier experiences were transmitted over space and time [R. F. Berkhofer Jr, 1964; R. A. Billington, 1966; H. N. Scheiber, 1969 b; G. W. Pierson, 1973]. Yet, having acknowledged such qualifications, Turner's thesis remains the best integrating scheme for analysing western history.

He produced a flexible document which can be timeless and boundless in its application if it is used in the inquiring spirit in which it was written. When Turner's general assertions on the importance of the frontier are treated as open-minded questions rather than definitive statements, the hypothesis takes on a pliable shape capable of being tested under most assumptions and with modern techniques [R. A. Billington, 1966; J. K. Putnam, 1976]. Turner's essay then becomes a pivot in historical research both for the framework it provides and the questions it poses, both explicitly and implicitly about the United States, and – by extension – about developing countries [M. W. Mikesell, 1960; M. T. Katzman, 1975; W. T. Jackson, 1976; A. Hennessey, 1978].

THE THESIS AND AMERICAN ECONOMIC HISTORY

While Turner's hypothesis encompassed the full dimensions of American history, the more limited question asked in this essay is, which frontier issues are relevant to an understanding of American economic history in the nineteenth century? From the perspective of the modern interest in growth and welfare, Turner's West can be viewed as a vast arena of free land and abundant resources waiting to be used by successive generations of native-born and foreign settlers. Defining the frontier in three distinct ways, firstly as a *condition* or as unused resources awaiting exploitation, secondly as a *process* of recurring stages of settlement, and finally as a specific *location* or geographic region, then the historian is in effect discussing growth in a newly settled area or the economics of under-development. The hypothesis must therefore be reformulated as a theory encompassing all strands of growth in an area undergoing new settlement.

THE FRONTIER AS CONDITION

Beginning with the frontier as a condition or in Turner's terms as 'the existence of an area of free land', historians analysing economic growth and welfare in the nineteenth century have focused on 'freeness'. Does free simply mean empty, or does it mean available at little or no cost, either to the pioneer as an individual, or to the country at large? The presence or absence of this freeness affects not only the shape and speed of resource utilisation, but also the distribution of assets and wealth in a democratic country.

If free is to be interpreted as the equivalent of vacant, Turner was incorrect. Given his Anglo-American perspectives he lumped the Native American in with the environment and further failed to appreciate any prior settlement where production for profit was not the major goal [D. A. Nichols, 1972; H. R. Lamar, 1973]. The cost of removing or controlling the Indians and also of formally acquiring a continental empire so that land could be freed and turned into public domain was taken for granted. In this Turner has not been alone. Economic historians in general have also neglected the antecedent occupation by non Anglo-American groups, and most assume that the millions of acres of western land came virtually costless to the federal government (pp. 21–6 below).

Was land free once the federal government took charge of the disposal policy? Clearly some settlers did not pay cash and others delayed payments. Most pioneers, however, bought their land, either from the government, or from a speculator, who, as a middleman, offered different sales' terms (see pp. 26–30 below). Even those individuals who were given land or who squatted temporarily, found that cash or credit was needed to turn their property into a valuable asset [P. W. Gates, 1968; C. H. Danhof, 1969] (see pp. 35–42 below). There was very little price-free land in an absolute sense. Nevertheless, in relative terms, when compared to the Old World, land was so cheap that cheapness became equated with free entry – at least in the eyes of millions of immigrants [B. Thomas, 1973].

Historians have paid considerable attention to the low price of lands, both for individual Americans as entrepreneurs, and for the growth potential of the United States. In discussing this issue they have concentrated on methods of land disposal. When the federal government adopted the free enterprise policy of selling land at the market price, rather than endowing a nation of small independent farm owners, or systematically controlling resource use, then it allowed intermediaries like the speculator and the moneylender to influence the speed and shape of economic growth through their control of developmental capital [R. P. Swierenga, 1977] (see pp. 29–30 below). If the government had insisted on democratic distribution, then it would have impeded free enterprise. Growth might then have been slower, but a more equitable distribution of wealth and more careful husbandry of exhaustible resources might have ensued [T. Le Duc, 1963 b].

The long-standing debate between the pro- and anti-capitalist historians on alternative policies of land distribution has recently been enlivened by the intervention of quantifiers with their statistical techniques. But their predictive models, even with strictly controlled specifications, are as subjective as the factual interpretations of their less numerate colleagues [R. W. Fogel and J. L. Rutner, 1972; R. T. Dennen, 1977]. The cheapness of Turner's lands continues to be a perennial bone of contention (see pp. 26–9 below).

Another debate centred on free or cheap lands asks whether the frontier provided a refuge for the oppressed. The direct 'safety-valve' mechanism whereby industrial wage-earners could migrate west in times of crises or depressions may not have worked, as Turner himself later acknowledged and generations of historians have subsequently proved [G. M. Gressley, 1958; R. A. Billington, 1973]. But the concept has been rejuvenated. When the entire frontier rather than the agrarian frontier is the safety-valve, then the West offers numerous opportunities by intensifying the demand for labour, increasing wages and alleviating possible social discontent [E. Von Nardroff, 1962; R. Hofstadter, 1968; J. K. Putnam, 1976]. The frontier may thus have had some beneficial social effects, though faster growth rates may have been impeded (see pp. 66–7 below).

THE FRONTIER AS PROCESS

When the frontier is defined as a process of development in which Turner's pioneers moved steadily westwards across the continent, then the economic historian seems, at first sight, to be faced with the subject of extensive growth. Geographical expansion and the exploitation of new resources suggest increased outputs from a larger base. Indeed better living standards might be obtained merely by expanding resources, but they are usually associated with efficiency arising from changes in technology and in organisation. The industrialising sector might thus be more significant for American development in the nineteenth century than were Turner's abundant natural resources [D. M. Potter, 1954; T. C. Cochran, 1975].

In following this line of argument historians do not often state that frontier expansion absorbed too much economic energy and severely retarded alternative patterns of growth [J. R. Williamson, 1974]. But they do now demand that the West must be considered in the context of an interdependent economy. Improvements in machine and transportation technology rapidly spread productivity gains to new areas and thus western growth was both extensive and intensive [D. C. North, 1961].

The Turnerian process of development is a static model in which the same stages of evolutionary growth are repeated throughout the West. But technological advances either accelerated or eliminated certain phases (see section 3, pp. 31–43 below). Better roads, steamboats, canals and then railroads ensured access to widespread markets, while new machinery, both on the farm and in the factory, raised productivity levels from reduced labour inputs [G. R. Taylor, 1951; J. G. Clark, 1966; W. N. Parker, 1971]. The ensuing commercial exploitation of primary resources ran counter to evolutionary stages and often brought concurrent rather than subsequent urban and industrial expansion [A. E. Fishlow, 1965; D. A. Smith, 1967] (see section 4, pp. 44–54 below).

Geography as well as technology further denied a uniform stage theory of growth. The unique location of mineral deposits and forest reserves, and the numerous variations in climate and landscape altered the timing and the duration of the phases of westward expansion (see sections 3 and 4, pp. 31–54 below). The frontier process of development in the nineteenth century revealed diversity rather than Turnerian conformity.

How then should the Frontier thesis be modified to meet these requirements? To become viable Turner's process must be rephrased as a question rather than read as a statement about the nature of economic growth in the West. Was the frontier settled in a series of stages through which man conquered the wilderness and gradually built up a mature society? Only a set of comparative studies can supply an answer. If the Turnerian pattern is viable in an area like the trans-Appalachian Plateau at the turn of the nineteenth century, then his framework of analysis can be applied to other areas to ascertain similar or divergent trends. A systematic scheme for measuring rates of growth and weighting factors of change can then be built into Turner's thesis. In this way comparisons and contrasts encompassing the broad 'time-space matrix' of the nineteenth century can be achieved without abandoning the original thesis.

THE FRONTIER AS LOCATION

The third facet of Turner's frontier, as a location, may also need to be redefined for modern usage (see pp. 56–7, 60 below). As a place

18

experiencing a low population density the frontier has been difficult to identify consistently over long periods of time. Historians have therefore tended to use the term as a pseudonym for virtually any newly settled area west of the Appalachian Mountains which has not attained economic maturity. They have thus introduced a general vagueness. Recently social scientists have called for greater precision and statistical accuracy in discussing frontier regions. They want to know firstly whether the original definition of two persons per square mile is an appropriate interpretation of underpopulation. If not, then what alternative should be adopted? They then proceed to ask which demographic phenomena contribute to retaining or altering frontier settlements [J. E. Eblen, 1965; J. E. Davis, 1977].

Despite the sophistication of new techniques the more recent demographic analyses of the structure of frontier society have not resolved these questions (see pp. 60–70 below). There has been little agreement on a uniform definition of frontier settlement. Then quantitative efforts to provide comparative case studies analysing population profiles have been disappointing. Certainly numerical evidence on relevant variables like place of birth, age, sex and occupation can be obtained from the manuscript schedules of the federal censuses taken at decennial intervals [M. Curti, et al., 1959; G. Blackburn and S. L. Richards Jr, 1970; D. J. Wishart, 1973]. But the choice of different-sized areas spanning diverse time-periods prevents sound comparisons. More disconcerting, however, are the efforts to categorise data to fit some modern or abstract theory not in keeping with the frontier context [R. K. Vedder and L. E. Galloway, 1975; J. E. Davis, 1977]. Indeed, faced at times by apparently irrelevant general demographic propositions, western historians may revert to the Census concept of two persons per square mile or to the temporal idea of the first generation of settlement. They may be satisfied to compromise by applying quantitative techniques and more sophisticated methods of analysis to any newly settled area where good qualitative sources provide supporting evidence. Systematic identification may not yet be possible and the frontier as a place may remain an enigma.

CONCLUSIONS

By focusing on the three concepts of frontier as condition, process and place, the economic historian can re-examine Turner's thesis to consider the pertinent questions about the development of the American West in the nineteenth century. Turner himself may not have envisaged the forms or the techniques of current research, but he did ask the basic questions –

namely — how the acquisition and disposal of abundant and good quality resources, and how the ensuing settlement patterns affected American economic growth.

2   Land, Its Abundance and Disposal

THE existence of millions of acres of free land, and by extension, abundant resources, is crucial to the economic significance of Turner's thesis because they provided opportunities for Americans both to improve their standards of living and to contribute to the rapid growth of the country. Academics who examine Turner's propositions about western lands ask about their nature, extent and availability. They have generally confirmed their presence, but have qualified their freeness and questioned the methods of disposal and acquisition.

THE EXTENT OF THE FRONTIER

If Turner's millions of acres are synonymous with the public domain, then there was certainly an available frontier for settlement. The public domain came into existence at the end of the Revolutionary Wars when leading Americans agreed that those seven of the original thirteen states claiming land beyond the Appalachian Mountains should yield their titles to the federal government [F. K. Van Zandt, 1966; P. W. Gates, 1968]. Initially this area stretched only to the Mississippi River and excluded the Floridas. But having gained confidence and strength during the early years of nationhood, Americans, both at the government and grass-roots levels, turned their attention to expanding their territorial domain. Through purchase, negotiation and annexation, of both the peaceful and belligerent varieties, the United States formally acquired some 1,808,000,000 acres of land by 1867 (see Table I and Map 1).

THE AVAILABILITY OF LAND

Was this vast expanse free? If free is defined either as vacant or unclaimed land, then the answer is no because there was settlement prior to American acquisition. When European nations first planted colonies in North America there may have been an aboriginal population of some 10,000,000. European diseases, colonial wars, intertribal warfare, alcohol

21

Table I

Acquisition of the Public Domain

Acquisition	Total area[1] (Acres)	Public Domain (Acres)	Cost (Dollars)	Cost per area of Public Domain (in Cents)
Area conceded to United States by Great Britain in 1783	495,850,880			
Ceded by seven states[2] to United States (1781–1802)	236,825,600	233,415,680	6,200,000	2.66
Louisiana Purchase (1803)	529,911,680	523,446,400	23,213,568	4.43
Red River Basin[3]	29,601,920	29,066,880	—	0.00
Cession from Spain (1819)	46,144,640	43,342,720	6,674,057	15.40
Annexation of Texas[4] (1845)	247,060,480			
Oregon Compromise (1846)	183,386,240	180,644,480	—	0.00
Mexican Cession (1848)	338,680,960	334,479,360	16,295,149	4.87
Purchase from Texas (1850)	78,926,720	78,842,880	15,496,448	19.65
Gadsden Purchase (1853)	18,988,800	18,961,920	10,000,000	52.74

Alaska Purchase (1867)	375,296,000	365,481,600	7,200,000	1.97
TOTAL PUBLIC DOMAIN	1,807,681,920		85,079,222	4.71[5]

NOTES: (1) Includes inland water; (2) Georgia Cession involved monetary transaction; (3) Authorities differ on the date of acquisition. Some think that it was part of the Louisiana Purchase, others think that it was acquired from Great Britain; (4) Texas retained control of its own public domain; (5) These figures are estimates, as sources differ on both acreage and costs.

SOURCE: Based on US Dept of Interior, *Public Land Statistics*, 1964 (Washington, DC, 1965).

CONTINENTAL EXPANSION OF THE UNITED STATES

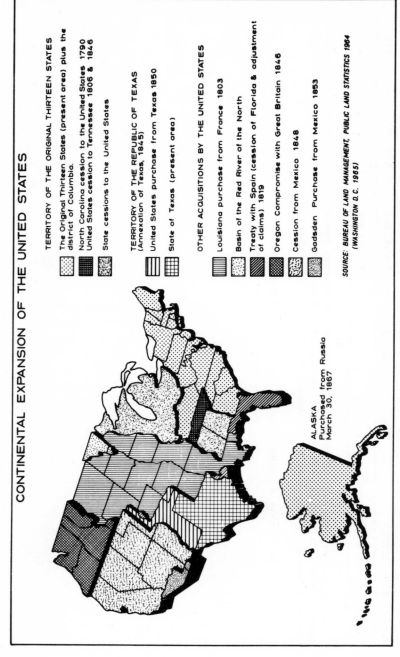

TERRITORY OF THE ORIGINAL THIRTEEN STATES

The Original Thirteen States (present area) plus the district of Columbia.

North Carolina cession to the United States 1790
United States cession to Tennessee 1806 & 1846

State cessions to the United States

TERRITORY OF THE REPUBLIC OF TEXAS
(Annexation of Texas, 1845)

United States purchase from Texas 1850

State of Texas (present area)

OTHER ACQUISITIONS BY THE UNITED STATES

Louisiana purchase from France 1803

Basin of the Red River of the North

Treaty with Spain (cession of Florida & adjustment of claims) 1819

Oregon Compromise with Great Britain 1846

Cession from Mexico 1848

Gadsden Purchase from Mexico 1853

SOURCE: BUREAU OF LAND MANAGEMENT, PUBLIC LAND STATISTICS 1964 (WASHINGTON D.C. 1965)

ALASKA
Purchased from Russia
March 30, 1867

MAP 1

and the disruption of traditional economic patterns, all contributed to substantial depopulation, and eventually a nadir of some 490,000 may have been reached in the early 1900s (H. F. Dobyns, 1966, 1976; C. A. Meister, 1976). Thus Indians must be given some numerical, let alone moral claim, to be considered as residents and possessors of the soil.

Even had Turner enjoyed the benefit of recent anthropological research on numbers, his free land, used as a synonym for unoccupied land would have remained the same. He recognised the existence of Native Americans, but they were part of his wilderness [D. A. Nichols, 1972]. They were at the lowest stage of societal evolution and would be eliminated by or become subservient to the superior Anglo-American civilisation and technology. Economic historians have generally followed Turner's example by paying little attention to aboriginal occupancy, but this state of affairs cannot continue.

Already American concern for minority rights and a growing awareness of alternative life-styles have stimulated new interpretations of many aspects of Indian–White relations [F. P. Prucha, 1976]. There are numerous scholarly accounts of particular tribes, trading relations, removal policies, Indian Wars and the management of reservations [F. P. Prucha, 1977]. Perhaps 'new' historians will now 'guestimate' the costs of disinheriting the Indians through quantifying hypothetical situations. It might be possible to ascertain alternative Gross National Products or growth rates if different policies had been adopted towards Indian land-holding. For those historians who only feel comfortable with facts, this model-building method may seem like fiction, but even they must acknowledge that the sums awarded in recent years, by the Indian Claims Commission, to tribes who gave up their aboriginal domain, are at very least, tentative modifications of the idea that lands were unoccupied and were thus free [N. O. Lurie, 1978].

Indians were not alone in claiming North American land. Spain, Holland, France, Britain and Russia had earlier established a colonial presence, and when the newly created United States looked west, it really replaced one brand of colonisation by another, softer variety. Americans justified their expansion in idealistic terms of spreading democracy and liberty, in addition to the traditional reasons of trade, economic growth and national defence [N. A. Graebner (ed.), 1968]. But whatever the motivation, territorial acquisition from other nations was not costless. Lands were not freely bestowed by some divine act of providence.

The expense of acquiring Turner's millions of acres was both monetary and psychological. At a purchase price of some 4.7 cents per acre, the federal government obtained a bargain (see Table I). But this cost does not include the military and administrative wages associated with occupation, negotiation and war. Of more significance, little attention has been given to the amounts expended by thousands of adventurous or dissident Americans who moved to foreign-held regions on the continent, and later actively sought admission, or what was euphemistically called readmission, into the United States. Discussed intellectually as agents of Manifest Destiny, or diplomatically as fifth columnists, these pioneers have been given little attention when considering whether lands were free, either in terms of being legally unclaimed or requiring no financial outlay [F. Merk, 1963; W. A. Williams, 1969]. Sophisticated theoretical models estimating their contributions might not greatly advance historical learning in this case, but any questioning of the cost of territorial expansion must cast doubts on the traditional assumptions that land was a 'given' economic factor in the growth of the nation.

LAND DISPOSAL POLICY

Historians have not neglected western lands once they were part of the public domain. Examinations of who had access to how much and under what circumstances have been both numerous and controversial. When the various state cessions of land gave the nation a public domain in the 1780s the federal government became one of the world's leading real estate agents (see Map 1). Decisions were then taken about land settlement and distribution. Two pieces of legislation, the Land Ordinance of 1785 and the Northwest Ordinance of 1787, formed the basis for the conduct of operations, both then and subsequently as the public domain was enlarged [R. M. Robbins, 1942; B. H. Hibbard, 1965; P. W. Gates, 1968]. Orderly settlement was essential. The 1787 Act set out the administrative framework for an evolutionary form of territorial government which would eventually ensure that new states obtained a status equal to that of the original thirteen. Political colonialism was a dead issue, though the actual territorial process involved many varieties of subservience [J. E. Eblen, 1968].

The 1785 Act provided for land disposal. When the Indian title had been cleared and the land surveyed it was to be sold at an auction to the highest bidder. A minimum price per acre and size of purchase unit was established. Though these figures varied in the course of the next century, no maxima were suggested. The open market system was not questioned and public control was never seriously considered [R. M. Robbins, 1942; B. H. Hibbard, 1965; P. W. Gates, 1968]. The government did not wish to monitor land usage. Indeed only late in the nineteenth century, following official classification and appraisal of public lands, did the government reluctantly bow to the pressure of scientists and conservationists to reserve land for national use and enjoyment [S. L. Udall, 1963; R. Nash, 1974]. Twentieth-century observers like to comment that this policy provided 'too little and too late', but they live in the midst of scarcity rather than abundance [W. R. Jacobs, 1978].

The free enterprise system allowed for various options. The government could either give or sell land to individuals, companies or institutions. Land was either donated in lieu of payment for services rendered, or as an incentive to encourage development. When it was sold, it provided a source of income for the treasury, but the price could influence the shape and speed of settlement. The contradictions in, and alterations to, land policy in the course of the nineteenth century, indicate both governmental indecision about national objectives and the strength of pressure groups in what was a democratic society [P. W. Gates, 1968; M. E. Young, 1969; P. W. Gates, 1976].

Initially, the need to refund debts incurred during the Revolution and the reluctance to find other sources of finance induced politicians to regard sales as a source of revenue for the federal government. Accordingly land was made available in large blocks at a minimum price of $1.00 per acre. As sales were slow the minimum purchase area was reduced, and though the price was doubled, credit provisions encouraged activity. The revenue influence gradually faded in importance in the early nineteenth century as the national debt was either retired or funded from alternative sources, but land sales were retained to ensure that superior lands would be used productively [D. C. North, 1966]. The income thus generated provided financial support for improvements in transportation or was redistributed back to the states [P. W. Gates, 1968, 1976].

As the revenue considerations of disposal declined, the federal government could be more liberal with its landed bounty. Yielding both to democratic and western pressures for cheaper land, the minimum purchase area was reduced. Then, in 1841, the general recognition of 'squatting' ahead of the official survey gave other would-be settlers the opportunity to buy their quarter-section of 160 acres at the minimum price, by applying capital accrued through their improvements before they obtained title to the land. The Graduation Act of 1854 scaled down the price of land according to the length of time it had been on the market. Meanwhile donations were granted to special groups like veterans or pioneers moving to remote areas like Florida or Oregon. Next, under the Homestead Act of 1862, it became possible to acquire

Table II

Disposition of Lands in the Public Domain 1789–1904

Type of Disposition	Area (In Acres)	Percentage of Total
Distributed Free[1]	120,227,824	6.64
Grants for construction of all[2] Transport Networks	127,262,717	7.03
Grants to States and Territories (For Resale)[3]	155,385,572	8.59
Cash Purchase	323,680,138	17.89
Reserved by the Government[4]	122,190,579	6.75
Indian Reservations	73,045,861	4.04
Unappropriated	841,872,377	46.52
Other[5]	45,874,772	2.54
Total Land Surface In Public Domain	1,809,539,840	100.00

NOTES: (1) Includes Indian Allotments, but not military bounties; (2) Includes Roads, Canals, Rivers, and Railroads; (3) Includes School and Swamp Land Acts; (4) Includes Federal and State Reserves and Reclamations; (5) Includes Mineral Lands, Private Claims, Scrip Lands, Agricultural College Lands.

SOURCE: Based on US 58 Cong. 3 Sess. Senate Documents, no 189, *Report* of the Public Lands Commission, 1905.

160 acres free in certain parts of the West [R. W. Robbins, 1942; B. H. Hibbard, 1965; P. W. Gates, 1968].

Turner's free lands – either in the sense of cash-free or very cheap – were becoming visible, but they did not provide the majority of acreage in the public domain (see Table II). Democratic liberality was counterbalanced by economic generosity designed to encourage development. Huge land grants were given to railroad corporations to construct networks and to state governments to support education. These intermediaries then sorted out high and low quality lands which they retailed at a 'real' market price. Other incentives to growth were offered in the late nineteenth century through legislation governing the cheap acquisition of timber and arid lands. Large sections of public domain were thus distributed directly or indirectly for promotional purposes [P. W. Gates, 1968; S. L. Engerman, 1972].

SPECULATION

The incongruity of American land disposal, however, does not lie simply in the dichotomy between democratic and developmental goals. By continuing sales at auctions and through land offices without restrictions on maximum purchases the federal government not only condoned, but favoured the presence of individual capitalists as real estate brokers. These middlemen, alongside the major grantees, were well placed to prescribe land prices and their role as speculators has long been the subject of debate [R. P. Swierenga, 1977].

Defined as any person who purchased more land than they themselves could use, speculators were traditionally regarded as parasites who made large profits by mere ownership and accumulated political power by mere presence. Tenancy, heavy tax burdens, poor farming techniques, political corruption, misuse of scarce capital, promoting inequality of wealth and retarding economic growth were among the main crimes of which the speculator was guilty [T. Le Duc, 1963 a; B. H. Hibbard, 1965; P. W. Gates, 1973]. Though some middlemen did encourage western settlement, they were generally deemed to have brought more harm than good.

This 'Progressive' attack on profit-making entrepreneurs has, however, been replaced by their acceptance and even welcome as providers of a necessary economic function. Several systematic studies, written in the 1950s and 1960s laid the foundations for the thesis that the success of western settlement depended on the presence of speculators [A. G. Bogue, 1955; A. G. and M. B. Bogue, 1957; H. M. Drache,

1964; R. P. Swierenga, 1968]. Indeed they were the essential planners in a planless society, for not only did they advertise lands and attract settlers, but they also provided credit and helped develop new communities — often through the payment of taxes. Certainly there were examples of fraud, chicanery and misjustice, but overall speculators aided rather than abetted settlement [P. W. Gates, 1968; R. P. Swierenga, 1977].

This pro-capitalist interpretation has been buttressed by cliometricians writing in the 1960s and 1970s. Armed with rigorous theoretical models and statistical techniques, these economists have examined the efficiency and equity effects of land speculation. From their quantitative perspective the real estate agent was an essential and effective part of American land market operations, speculation neither retarded nor accelerated growth, and its impact on wealth distribution may also have been minimal [D. C. North, 1966; R. W. Fogel and J. L. Rutner, 1972; E. H. Rastatter, 1975; L. Soltow, 1979]. In other words, modern research suggests that Americans provided themselves with as efficient and as good a land disposal mechanism as was possible in a democratic free enterprise nation in the nineteenth century.

3   Agricultural Development

ACQUISITION of land is not the only ingredient in ascertaining the economic significance of Turner's millions of acres. Developmental costs are critical in considering how pioneers turned the wilderness into a productive area. If opportunity existed in abundance then the millions of settlers who moved west to farm must have been able to build up successful enterprises.

THE PROCESS OF AGRICULTURAL CHANGE

Most western farmers wished to acquire land to improve their economic state. Turner certainly envisaged this materialistic objective and did not endow his pioneers with the philosophical ideal of self-sufficiency in a rural utopia. But the unfolding of Turner's agrarian frontier was slow. The initial use of land on an extensive basis for cattle grazing was followed by a thinly scattered and temporary subsistence farming. The more permanent settler who came next used the soil intensively and raised some crops for sale. He in turn was succeeded by the moneyed entrepreneur who participated fully in the market economy. This evolutionary process was repeated as settlers moved west and thus Turner provided a static model of development, apparently stressing the values of agrarianism [F. J. Turner, 1893] (see p. 11 above).

Recent scholars have been concerned to convert this static model into a dynamic approach which can encompass the diversity of early western farming patterns [A. G. Bogue, 1963; J. G. Clark, 1966; C. H. Danhof, 1969; R. D. Mitchell, 1977]. At first sight their phases of expansion look like new-fangled versions of Turner's stages. The first phase of complete self-sufficiency and marginal living standards is followed by a period of unspecialised farming and local commercialism. The third level of agricultural specialisation and increasing commercialism is finally over-taken by agricultural regionalisation and participation in national and international markets [R. D. Mitchell, 1977]. The differences, however, are more basic than those of language, for the length of each farming phase can vary according to time and location. They can be of very short or long duration. Two might coexist within the same local area, or two or more might be compressed as farmers took advantage of improved conditions. Thus the modern interpretation of the farmers' frontier is a flexible process capable of incorporating innovations rather than being a repetitive pattern moving across the continent.

The speed with which pioneers turned their farms into business enterprises depended on geography, technology and capital availability. Agricultural frontiers were established at different times and in varying physical environments, or what might be called a constantly changing 'time-space matrix'. Settlers who acquired farms in the late nineteenth century might rapidly make them productive thanks to improved machinery, scientific knowledge and easy access to markets. But their ability and willingness to participate fully in a commercial system depended on their assessment of developmental costs. Many farmers lacked liquid funds and were already carrying a mortgage on their property. They were only likely to borrow more capital if the price of farm commodities suggested reasonable profits. Furthermore their farms had specific locations and geographical elements which had to be considered, including not only soil, topography, vegetation, climate and water availability, but also distance from markets and trading networks. There was no repetitive process of farming frontiers expanding west-wards. Instead there was a series of diverse local and regional adjustments.

ALTERNATIVE HISTORICAL APPROACHES TO PIONEER FARMING

In reformulating Turner's static approach to farming into a set of commercial responses in a developing, but unpredictable, economy, three alternative methods of analysis are available. The first and more conventional approach divides the country into crop-growing regions at specific periods and then examines important elements of change. This provides ample data on the growth and improvement of agriculture on a macro-level, but the discussion of patterns of pioneer farming are submerged in the general overview [L. C. Gray, 1933; P. W. Bidwell and J. I. Falconer, 1925 (repr. 1941); F. A. Shannon, 1945; P. W. Gates, 1960].

Secondly, innovative work has focused on specific elements which transformed a self-sufficient farm into a business operation. Some valuable insights on the introduction and diffusion of machine tech-nology, the backwards and forwards linkages of transport networks, the efficiency of financial intermediaries and the human investment in education, have broadened the narrow perspectives of many western historians [C. H. Golembe, 1952; D. C. North, 1956, 1961; A. E. Fishlow, 1965; P. A. David, 1966 (repr. 1971); C. H. Danhof, 1969; H. N. Scheiber, 1969 a; R. V. Scott, 1970; J. Mak, E. F. Haites and G. M. Walton, 1975; A. L. Olmstead, 1975; A. G. Bogue, 1976]. But the different methods used and the fragmentary nature of much of this research leaves many questions about the frontier unasked, let alone unanswered.

THE CASE-STUDY APPROACH (see Map 2)

(Readers should note that these case-study areas are only part of a larger geographical region which was settled under similar circumstances. Thus the areas marked on Map 2 as the 'Far West' are only the location of three case studies *within* the Far West, and are by no means co-terminous with the whole of that immense region.)

The third and most substantial body of information on pioneer agriculture can be found in local history. Though most commemorative and biographical volumes are too parochial to document a general discussion of early farming, there are many informative monographs which have been written within relevant analytical frameworks. A sample of these studies providing a range of comparative experiences within the time-space matrix of the West in the nineteenth century offers the best method of revisiting Turner's agricultural frontiers.

The wooded Appalachian Plateau country was the first focus of attention by pioneer farmers in the post-Revolutionary era. Here it is possible to see Turner's evolutionary stages in action, though better access to markets was already accelerating the transition to commercialisation. The next generation of newcomers fanned out in various directions – as shall be seen in the case studies of particular parts of the Midwestern prairies the Gulf area and the Far West.

Those farmers on the continuous moving frontier of the mid-century who took advantage of new modes of transport and of improvements in machinery and crop strains, were well placed to participate in a market economy if they could adapt to their geographical and institutional environments. Their contemporaries who leap-frogged to and beyond the Rocky Mountains found that their commercial potential was not only altered by arid and at times hostile surroundings, but was limited to areas tributary to the Pacific. Later in the nineteenth century when settlers moved on to the Northern Plains and filled in the North Central area,

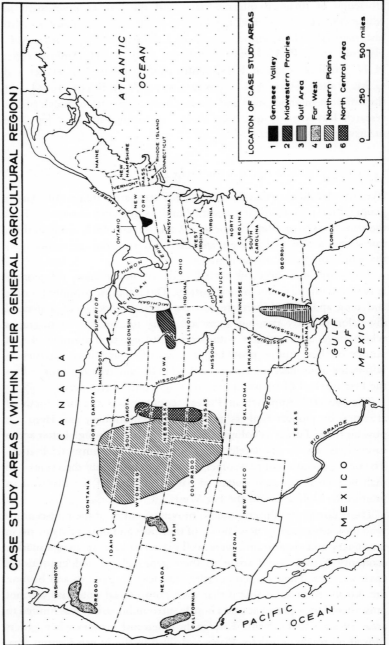

CASE STUDY AREAS (WITHIN THEIR GENERAL AGRICULTURAL REGION)

LOCATION OF CASE STUDY AREAS

1 Genesee Valley
2 Midwestern Prairies
3 Gulf Area
4 Far West
5 Northern Plains
6 North Central Area

0   250   500 miles

MAP 2

34

technology provided agricultural implements and access to markets. But often tools had to be modified to suit specific locations which were frequently marginal in economic terms. In addition, charges absorbed profits, and commodity prices fell in a saturated world market. As good lands became scarcer, the frontier acceptance of commercialism was more painful than profitable, as the farm protest movements of the time signified. By the turn of the twentieth century little pioneer farming remained.

(i) *The Genesee Valley*

As American farmers pushed west across the Appalachian Mountains in the late eighteenth and early nineteenth centuries they moved gradually out of a stage of self-sufficiency to one of semi-subsistence and local commercialism [R. C. Loehr, 1952; R. Horsman, 1970]. In the undulating wooded prairies of the fertile Genesee Valley of upstate New York, a pioneer of the 1790s was highly self-supporting, since it took several years of backbreaking toil before he could clear enough acreage to raise crops for sale. Animals were kept either for consumption or as a work force. Corn was the basic cereal crop because it needed little preparation of the land, could be easily harvested over a long period and provided both human and animal food. Other crops for home use might include vegetables, and flax or wool for clothing [N. A. McNall, 1952; J. Van Wagenen Jr, 1953].

Yet even this Turnerian farmer, whether he remained for several years or moved on rapidly, needed money to pay for metal tools, kitchen utensils and essential food items like salt, sugar and coffee. To obtain these he had to raise some marketable crops. As road and water transport was slow, seasonal and expensive, he looked for local sales of bulky commodities to newcomers moving into the Genesee Valley or to settlers in Upper Canada. Alternatively high value and non-perishable crops like potash, whisky, hemp, maple syrup or marino wool could bear transport costs to distant markets, as could cattle driven on the hoof. But wheat, which would grow well once the land was cleared, was too expensive to move, even when milled into flour. The Genesee Valley farmer at the turn of the nineteenth century faced limited prospects [N. A. McNall, 1952; R. Horsman, 1970; R. A. Billington, 1974].

Improvements in transport could extend market thresholds. Better roads alleviated some short-haul problems. Then when the Erie Canal was opened in 1825 and freight rates from Buffalo to New York City fell from $100.00 to $12.00 a ton, long-distance trade with and through New

35

York City became viable and Genesee farmers planted more wheat [G. R. Taylor, 1951; N. A. McNall, 1952; R. E. Shaw, 1966]. New and improved ploughs, cultivators and threshing-machines helped increase outputs, but harvesting with a scythe or cradle, and threshing with a flail or early fanning mill still created bottlenecks and required a pool of migratory labour [L. Rogin, 1931; N. A. McNall, 1952; C. H. Danhof, 1969]. Yet by the early 1830s enough progress had been made for the Genesee Valley to be known as the 'Granary of America'. In the space of some 40–50 years Turner's farming frontiers had passed through the region.

(ii) The Midwestern Prairies

The capacity for telescoping stages of pioneer farming was greatly enhanced by the diffusion of technology in the quarter-century before the Civil War. Major improvements in farm machinery and the construction of intra- and inter-regional transport networks enlarged market potential [P. W. Gates, 1960; J. G. Clark, 1966; C. H. Danhof, 1969; R. A. Billington, 1974]. The speed with which pioneers responded to these opportunities was related to the ecological conditions and locations of their farms, their skills in procuring capital and in utilising new implements, their family size, plant varieties and livestock, and the flexibility of marketing institutions [C. H. Danhof, 1969]. Not all farmers reacted rapidly, but in the antebellum era many realised that their success was increasingly measured in terms of maximising money income rather than in acres devoted to family consumption. Turner's frontiersmen were becoming risk-taking businessmen.

Midwestern pioneers illustrate the speed and diffusion of commercial farming. Moving first on to the open prairies of Illinois, southern Wisconsin and Iowa in the mid-1830s and early 1840s, they faced ecological conditions of humid but sparsely wooded grassland. Adjustments to timber shortage required some substitutions in buildings, fencing and fuel, while breaking the densely matted prairie sod required special equipment [L. Rogin, 1931; P. W. Gates, 1960; A. G. Bogue, 1963; C. H. Danhof, 1969; D. E. Schob, 1975].

Once in production, however, the land was very fertile and either wheat or corn could be profitably raised according to climatic variations. Small towns provided early local markets. Then for those farmers situated near the major waterway systems of the Mississippi River or the Great Lakes, long-distance shipments were economically viable. Corn raisers often fed their crop to the more transportable hog which was then processed into pork for shipment downriver [M. Walsh, 1978]. The more northerly wheat farmers meanwhile sought reduced freight costs through the construction of plank roads to Lake ports [C. Abbott, 1971]. Progress was more rapid in the late 1840s and the 1850s because new ploughs, reapers, threshers and harvesters boosted outputs, improved breeding and made livestock more palatable, while western railroads opened up markets for previously landlocked areas. Frontier farm-making became increasingly market-focused and profit-motivated from the very start, without waiting to go through Turner's stages [P. W. Gates, 1960; A. E. Fishlow, 1965; J. G. Clark, 1966; C. H. Danhof, 1969].

Turner and many other historians might argue, however, that not all midwestern pioneers could become commercial farmers, for even though technology provided solutions to production problems, these solutions cost money which the settler did not have. Here management skills and institutional arrangements must be considered. Those farmers with capital bought machinery as it became a practical economic proposition. Those hampered by debt for land purchase followed suit at a slower pace: they minimised cost by gradual expansion, hiring out work and sharing equipment or buying machinery on credit extended either by the manufacturer, relatives or financial intermediaries [A. G. Bogue, 1963; M. Walsh, 1972; A. L. Olmstead, 1975]. Indeed borrowing capital was not merely legitimate; it was positively necessary. Farmers might dislike debts, but they were part of their way of life. When yields were good and prices were high, credit was often responsible for success. The converse equally applied. General financial crises, poor harvests or prices, and high interest rates could bring bankruptcy. Commercialism involved risks, but midwestern pioneers were increasingly willing to take these risks to maximise productivity [M. Throne, 1949; A. G. Bogue, 1963; C. H. Danhof, 1969]. They were unwilling to evolve slowly through Turnerian stages.

(iii) *The Gulf Region*

Did pioneers in the Gulf States of Alabama and Mississippi experience the same process of modernisation in the antebellum years? Certainly the physical environment offered economic potential. Land was abundant, soils were fertile and climate favoured the growth of several crops. Corn was raised everywhere, either for home consumption or for sale locally. Cotton was the most widespread cash crop, while sugar and rice provided limited alternatives [L. C. Gray, vol. 2, 1933; P. W. Gates, 1960; R. A. Billington, 1974; M. J. Rohrbough, 1978]. Farm commodities could be moved cheaply by water to coastal markets, but wagon-freighting to rivers was slow and expensive. Some of these land difficulties were alleviated by railroad construction in the 1850s [M. J. Rohrbough, 1978; J. F. Stover, 1978]. There was thus opportunity for newcomers in the Gulf West to become commercial farmers provided they had developmental capital.

In contrast to the contemporary Midwest this capital was invested in unfree black labour rather than in machinery. The institution of slavery thereby made southern farming frontiers peculiar. Indeed many historians would argue that new farming experiences in the Gulf region should be analysed as part of the transmission of southern civilisation rather than that of westward expansion [E. D. Genovese, 1965; W. N. Parker (ed.), 1970; M. J. Rohrbough, 1978]. It is certainly impossible to avoid discussing the economic and social values associated with the plantation, for they not only involved the basic distinction between slavery and freedom, but they also brought disparities of wealth and status to the frontier. Owners of plantations, of whatever size, who purchased land for immediate cotton raising, so as to utilise their investment in slaves, were not Turnerian pioneers, and the rapid expansion of the frontier in Alabama and Mississippi was built round the commercial production of cotton for European and North-eastern markets [L. C. Gray, vol. 2, 1933; R. A. Billington, 1974; M. J. Rohrbough, 1978]. The plantation here must be regarded as a different variant of pioneer agriculture.

How did the existence of large-scale operations using slave labour affect the numerous small-scale frontier farmers in the same area? They frequently bought land of poorer quality since good cotton-growing areas commanded a high price. As unspecialised farmers they retained a relatively high degree of self-sufficiency and raised some crops commercially. If they were skilled managers they gradually planted more acres under cotton and even acquired slaves, so that they came to build up a plantation – which can be considered as a larger farm, or a way of life, or both. But most simply held their own because frontier society was stratified, their lands were less fertile and they could not compete with plantation owners for developmental capital [F. Linden, 1946; F. L. Owsley, 1949; M. J. Rohrbough, 1978]. Here in the Gulf area the frontier was peculiar in its process of settlement and style of growth.

(iv) *The Far West*

Further diversity was visible in the antebellum Far West. Pioneers who moved hundreds of miles ahead of the continuous line of settlement shared a common geographical problem of distance, in that whatever level of production they achieved, their market threshold was limited because it was tributary to the Pacific coast region. Crops were sold locally or intra-regionally because high freight charges prevented long-distance movement of all but exotic produce. Farmers might be capable of responding to commercial pressures, but until the operation of the trans-continental railroads in the 1870s and 1880s they could not participate effectively in the national economy [E. Pomeroy, 1965; G. C. Fite, 1966].

Within the Far West, however, markets fluctuated and pioneer farming further reflected different natural and institutional environments. In California, prior Mexican settlement entailed initial uncertainty both in terms of access to and price of land [D. Hornbeck, 1976]. But when, in the 1850s, American pioneers used machinery to farm the flat fertile middle sections of the Central Valley, they rapidly made substantial beginnings, primarily in wheat but also in fruits, vegetables and livestock. The combination of favourable landscape, benign climate, available capital in the form of gold, river shipments of crops and rapid population growth, produced a remarkable farming frontier full of commercial drive, though with limited demand potential [R. W. Paul, 1947, 1973; P. W. Gates, 1967].

The valley settlements of Oregon were a pale image of the Californian experience. The terrain and climate, though different, certainly favoured the raising of cereals, fruits and livestock [J. Schafer, 1938; D. W. Meinig, 1968; W. A. Bowen, 1978]. But even after the influx of the Gold Rush population at midcentury, markets were small. Oregon farmers could not compete with the rising productivity and better location of their Californian counterparts. Then, the cost of freighting produce by packhorse or wagon across the mountains to interior transient mining camps, was frequently too expensive to be viable and ocean shipments to eastern parts of the United States were also prohibitive. Geographical isolation and the lack of effective land transport impeded farming prospects [J. Schafer, 1938; D. W. Meinig, 1968].

The Mormons, who had deliberately isolated themselves in a hostile environment in Utah in the late 1840s, illustrate yet another type of Far Western pioneer. They farmed according to the individual's ability to use land and they worked on a co-operative basis to irrigate the arid terrain [L. J. Arrington, 1958]. Aiming at self-sufficiency, crops were initially raised to guarantee the permanence of the Great Basin Kingdom. Soon, however, sales of produce and livestock to migrants on the overland trails offered a ready-made and unexpected market which was enlarged by those miners who moved inland in the 1850s and 1860s [L. J. Arrington, 1958; R. W. Paul, 1963; J. D. Unruh Jr, 1979]. Though the early farm outputs of a desert environment were not economically competitive with those of better endowed regions, the geography of Utah as a transport corridor created an unforeseen demand. Pioneer farming in Utah neither evolved in stages, nor was determined by environment.

(v) *The Northern Plains*

If farming frontiers in the years before the Civil War offer a range of experiences which do not readily substantiate a static model of development, then their counterparts in the late nineteenth century point to still other modifications. Commercialised agriculture was essential to survival, but the benefits of improved farm machinery and better access to markets by rail were offset by the difficulties of belonging to an organised and impersonal national economy, and of participating in international trade. Add to these considerations the problems arising from another set of environmental adjustments as settlers pushed beyond the 98th meridian, which roughly marked the boundary of aridity for intensive farming, then Turner's agricultural stages become even more difficult to identify [F. A. Shannon, 1945; G. C. Fite, 1966; E. Dick, 1975].

Two varieties of farming – livestock-raising and crop-raising – flourished in the new West in the post Civil War years. In this respect Turner rightly identified a pattern of extensive followed by more intensive land use – a pattern which had also been visible in the Ohio Valley, the Midwestern Prairies, Oregon and Texas [W. P. Webb, 1931; R. G. Clelland, 2nd edn, 1951; P. C. Henlein, 1959; J. E. Oliphant, 1968; P. W. Gates, 1973]. The cattle frontier of the High Plains emerged in the late 1860s and early 1870s when entrepreneurs realised that animals could withstand the severe winters and could graze both freely and safely on the open range following the pacification of the Indians. Taking advantage of new railroads to ship cattle to central markets where they commanded a good price, livestock farming on the Northern Plains was a commercial venture from the start. As overhead costs were low and early profits were high, both Eastern and European capital flowed west, often through formal investment channels [E. E. Dale, 2nd ed., 1960; L. Atherton, 1961; G. M. Gressley, 1966].

Expansion was rapid in the 1870s and early 1880s but the boom was short-lived as the range became overstocked and markets became saturated. Farmers also competed to use the land for raising cereals and then extreme weather conditions in the mid-1880s brought crippling losses [W. P. Webb, 1931; E. E. Dale, 2nd ed., 1960]. The saga of the 'Cattle Kingdom' has captured the imagination of western novelettes and the mass media, but despite the romantic gloss this livestock frontier was always a business enterprise. There was no self-sufficient stage even in the early years when rampant individualism flourished, and soon the organisation of cattlemen's associations signalled an awareness of modern interdependent world trading relations. Even ranchers eventually had to rationalise their operations on the model of the large corporation [E. E. Dale, 2nd edn, 1960; L. Atherton, 1961; G. M. Gressley, 1966].

(vi) The North Central Area

Cattle ranchers did not have undisputed claim to the land west of the 98th meridian in the 1870s and 1880s, as farmers also wished to settle on the flat, treeless, water-deficient expanses of the Plains and engage in commercial operations as quickly as possible. But their economic and physical environment called for new as well as old responses. The geography of grain growing in this region – frequently called the Great American Desert – entailed more natural hazards than on earlier frontiers. The vast stretches of flat or rolling grassland might be advantageous, but absence of trees entailed shortage of building materials and fuel. More important, however, from the settlers' perspective, insufficient rainfall, together with high winds, made cereal raising at best marginal, at worst disastrous [G. C. Fite, 1966; E. Dick, 1975].

Many of these problems had technological solutions. The introduction of barbed wire and better windmills lessened fencing and water deficiency difficulties, while improved farm machinery increased productivity and allowed new methods of cultivation. Crop genetics furnished strains more suited to the aridity and growing seasons of the Plains, and educational and government agencies spread information about innovations. Then distance from markets was alleviated by the construction of transcontinental railroads and feeder lines [W. P. Webb, 1931; F. A. Shannon, 1945; G. C. Fite, 1966].

The conquest of the natural environment was never complete, however, as pioneers had to learn from hard experience that farming on the Plains was risky and expensive. Wells, windmills and equipment for dry farming only provided partial remedies to aridity, but drought entailed crop failures and subsequent bankruptcy. Then neither technology nor institutional arrangements could prevent other natural disasters like grasshopper plagues, fires and storms [J. C. Malin, 1936; H. E. Briggs, 1950; G. C. Fite, 1966; E. Dick, 1975].

Of more importance, the decline in wholesale agricultural prices in both national and world markets meant that the economic returns from farming were falling. Plains farmers, already in debt for land purchase, lacked the capital or credit to obtain new equipment from a smaller real income, but even increased outputs provided no solution since they entailed further borrowing and aggravated the general problem of abundant staple commodities [J. D. Hicks, 1931; F. A. Shannon, 1945]. Moreover declining wholesale prices were not the farmers' only problem. Railroads and mercantile firms both levied charges for their services, which were now essential to participate in an economy increasingly organised in large units [M. Rothstein, 1969; J. Lurie, 1972]. The economic environment of the Plains' farmers seemed more hostile than the semi-arid natural environment, as they struggled against debt and destitution.

Certainly the agrarian protest movements of the late nineteenth century illustrate the range of problems for pioneers striving to adjust to an organised international market in which American farm products were declining in importance. Economic historians still question how far farmers' complaints were misguided and how much they merely resented being totally rather than partially commercialised [J. D. Hicks, 1931; D. C. North, 1966; A. Mayhew, 1972]. Social and political historians broaden the debate and ask whether farmers were irrational about their declining status in an industrial nation, or whether they were put in the position of being harbingers of a new style of government-managed society [J, D. Hicks, 1931; R. Hofstadter, 1955]. But on whatever grounds the academic debate is conducted, the protests do signal the closing of the farming frontier. Certainly many pockets of the West still remained unoccupied, but these were frequently marginal unless irrigated or used for grazing. Most of the desirable lands on the public domain were gone when Turner presented his thesis.

Conclusions

The case-study approach to frontier farming suggests diversity rather than similarity in the process of settlement. Turner's repetitive pattern of evolutionary stages is not visible in the broad time-space matrix to which it has been applied. But this does not mean that his thesis must be abandoned in the context of the frontier as process (see pp. 17−18 above). If his propositions are turned into questions rather than the dogmatic

42

statements proposed by some of his followers, then these suggestions can be used constructively. Fitting the Turnerian scheme to a suitable location like the Genesee Valley in the early nineteenth century, then the historian can measure change in other areas and at other times by ascertaining the degree of participation in a commercial economy. If the same questions are asked about the speed and intensity of farm improvements and the proportion of crops sold in markets in a variety of frontier areas, then the process of agricultural settlement can be discussed as part of an interdependent economy. Turner's scheme will provide the jumping-off point for as many case studies as is deemed essential to understand agricultural development in newly settled areas.

4   Other Stages of Early Western Growth

TURNER'S evolutionary model encompassed other varieties of natural resource use and the development of towns and industries as well as farming frontiers (see p. 11 above). Discussion of these other stages of early western growth has proceeded at varying rates along diverse paths. The spearheads — or first waves — of frontier exploitation have attracted contrasting interpretations. Romantic and semi-popular historians have revelled in the deeds of adventurous individuals who flourished in the wilderness. Their economic counterparts have suggested that most of these persons were often a small link in a large organised business. At the end of the frontier process the urban and commercial aspects, neglected in traditional approaches, have recently received considerable attention from the 'new' urban and economic historians. These different strands of research must be examined in any reassessment of the Turner thesis.

THE FUR TRADE

According to Turner the first Euro-American pioneers to venture west were the hunters, traders and trappers. Blazing trails across the vast interior these 'agents of civilization' prepared the way for later pioneers (see Map 3). Romantic historians reinforced the image of the heroic 'fur man' both in the Great Lakes Region in the Revolutionary Era, and on the Upper Missouri and in the Rockies in the 1820s and 1830s. The adventures of this latter group — the Mountain Men — are often regarded as the most exciting in the history of the frontier because they manfully grappled with the untamed forces of nature, conquering yet at the same time being moulded by their environment. These 'white savages' who gloried in anarchic freedom were men of action and few words. They lived rough and died young [J. A. Hawgood, 1967; H. R. Lamar, 1977; W. H. Goetzman, 1978].

While romantic interpretations have made the fur trader generally, and the Mountain Men in particular, superb subjects for escapism, their economic importance needs realistic assessment. They may well have

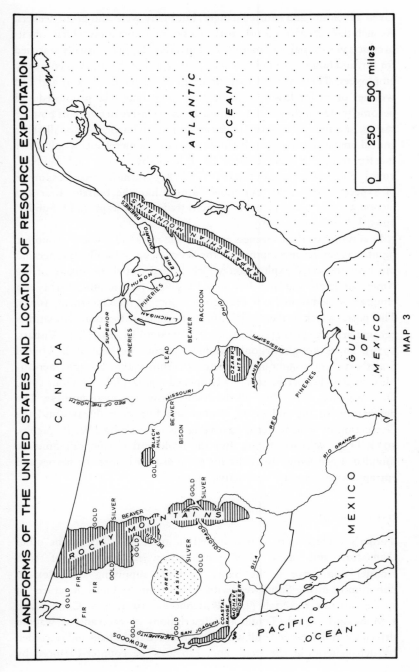

LANDFORMS OF THE UNITED STATES AND LOCATION OF RESOURCE EXPLOITATION

MAP 3

0   250   500 miles

45

loved adventure and courted danger, but many were also profit-seekers. As such they were frequently part of a business operation which sold its products in national and international markets. Trappers usually searched for fur, and hunters for hides or skins, either as free agents, or as company employees. They worked long hours in primitive conditions and bad weather often for low reward or pay. They might be promoted and become traders if they could administer an extensive network of posts or camps, or if they accumulated sufficient capital to finance part or all of the annual operations. Frequently, however, outside merchants would enter the fur trade and take control [R. E. Oglesby, 1967; D. J. Wishart, 1979]. The beaver trade of the 1820s and 1830s furnishes many examples of expectant capitalists, but other animals like the buffalo, bear and racoon also provided pelts for western traders and trappers [J. Sunder, 1965; J. L. Clayton, 1966].

In addition to their business activities fur men had a wider economic significance in the development of the West. Geographically, trappers did much of the early exploration which helped dispel the image of the American desert, and later they served as guides both to official army and emigrant expeditions [J. A. Hawgood, 1967; W. H. Goetzman, 1978]. The posts which traders established at strategic locations sometimes became army depots and the nucleii of western towns [D. J. Wishart, 1979]. Then, though furs only produced about 1 per cent of the United States' exports throughout the nineteenth century, they brought mercantile capital and expertise to a newly opened region [J. L. Clayton, 1966; D. J. Wishart, 1979]. Not all the results, however, were positive. The debilitation of the Indian by alcohol and European diseases and the destruction of wild life are negative facets of trapping [W. R. Jacobs, 1970; D. J. Wishart, 1979]. But the ecological clarion call must be sounded much louder to revise fur trade history before the heroes and entrepreneurs become 'destructive varmints'.

OTHER TRADE

Turner's traders were also involved in mercantile operations other than furs and skins. The most renowned example of such frontier commerce is the Santa Fe trade supplying the Mexican community in the Southwest with goods from St Louis in return for specie and raw materials [J. D. Rittenhouse, 1971; S. V. Connor and J. M. Skaggs, 1977]. Traditional descriptions of caravans of wagons driven by muleteers and bull whackers, attacked by Indians and rewarded by debaucheries at the trail's end, can now be counter-balanced by economic analyses of the 'commerce of the prairies'. Starting from a modest base in the early 1820s the trade realised high if irregular returns on investment for nearly twenty years. Furthermore, considerable secondary benefits accrued from building up a long-distance freighting business, from processing Mexican raw materials into consumer goods and from advertising weak Mexican control over its northern provinces [J. D. Rittenhouse, 1971; S. V. Connor and J. M. Skaggs, 1977]. Though this interpretation may smack of economic imperialism, other examples of a mercantile penetration of frontier regions from entrepôts as varied as New York, Philadelphia, Pittsburgh or Cincinnati merely form part of a world-wide search for new resources and markets [J. E. Vance, 1970] (see pp. 25–6 above and p. 51 below).

MINING

Two other 'cutting edges', the miners and the lumbermen, followed the traders and trappers in early western development. These transient pioneers were part of a geographically dispersed frontier whose location and duration were dictated by the presence of valuable resources (see Map 3). Despite their irregular appearance in the traditional accounts of westward expansion, their economic importance is such that they must be included in any reassessment of the significance of the frontier.

Some miners, like the numerous 'Forty-Niners' who rushed to California to 'strike it rich', are well known. Novels, popular history, songs and films have portrayed adventure, excitement and even glamour in the over-crowded camps and shanty-towns of the 'Golden Land of Opportunity'. But the mineral frontier was more important than the flush days of 1849. The continuation of gold-mining in California, the exploitation of precious metals in the Mountain West in the 1850s and ensuing decades, or even the earlier lead diggings in the Upper Mississippi Valley in the 1830s and 1840s, offer dimensions beyond escapism and the Turnerian approach of steady westward expansion [J. Schafer, 1932; R. W. Paul, 1947, 1963].

Early arrivals in California were lucky enough to find placer gold eroded from its natural vein and deposited by stream flows either in river beds or on hillsides. Little skill, equipment or capital was needed to dig for this gold or to separate it from the surrounding gravel. Modest fortunes could easily be made. They were even more easily lost by paying high prices for imported merchandise and through gambling and prostitution. The early strikes, however, were short-lasting, and placer deposits in the Sierra foothills were rapidly exhausted as the numbers of would-be miners mushroomed from 5000 in late 1848 to 40,000 a year later and then to 100,000 in 1852 [R. W. Paul, 1947, 1963].

Californian miners then faced three choices. They could join the work force of a company, find another local occupation or move elsewhere in search of mineral wealth. As quartz mining became more important in California in the mid 1850s, companies were formed to provide the capital, technology and organisation required to extract gold at depth [R. W. Paul, 1947, 1963]. Outputs continued to flow providing a firm foundation for local development and contributing largely to the American mint [R. W. Paul, 1947, 1963; T. S. Berry, 1976]. But gold digging ceased to be an adventure as miners became day-labourers. Then many migrants took up farming or moved into commerce and manufacturing which had rapidly emerged in the towns serving the gold-fields. Indeed California offered a wide range of opportunities to those who wished to stay [R. W. Paul, 1947; R. Mann, 1972; R. W. Lotchin, 1974].

The other disillusioned miners who were still infected with gold fever reversed the normal direction and moved east in search of precious minerals (see Map 3). Some joined rushes to the Fraser River in British Columbia in the late 1850s and then moved to Idaho and Montana in the early 1860s. Others made discoveries in Nevada and Arizona, while still others travelled further to link up with the westward-moving 'Fifty-Niners' in the Pike's Peak region of Colorado [R. W. Paul, 1963]. Many of these Rocky Mountain strikes based on vein or lode deposits required large-scale, highly capitalised enterprise. This brought both employment on a company pay-roll and more permanent settlement. The Mountain West thus experienced a frontier development focused on scattered towns which were serviced by an improving transport network and some subsidiary farming [C. C. Spence, 1958; W. S. Greever, 1963; D. A. Smith, 1967]. Given this perspective, historians have, not surprisingly, modified Turner's agrarian and Midwestern-oriented thesis (see pp. 11 − 14 above).

LUMBERING

Lumbering adds yet another component to the economic vanguard of the frontier. Like mining, the westward expansion of forestry was geographically scattered and timber exploitation often encouraged an urban-based rather than an agricultural pattern of growth. As with mining and trapping, lumbering also attracted adventurous individuals whose heroic deeds live on in folk history, but whose existence depended on being paid by a company selling in regional and national markets. Unlike its analagous spearheads, however, logging has received little general attention. Despite his Wisconsin background, Turner neglected lumbering. There are no plaid-shirted loggers with knitted toque, calked boots and double-bitted axe in his progress of civilisation [D. C. Smith, 1974]. Subsequent generations of western interpreters have also ignored the exploitation of timber resources, and the information available in local monographs still awaits synthesis.

Lumbering as a pattern of frontier development focused primarily on three areas (see Map 3). In the early national period the forests of western New England and of backstate New York and Pennsylvania supplied the construction requirements of the North east, but by the 1830s these resources had been denuded. Loggers then explored the pineries of the Great Lakes which they 'cut' piecemeal in the 1830s and 1840s. In the following decades Midwestern lumbering became more systematic and corporations sold timber in the emerging national market, but the cut-and-move-on mentality invariably brought debris and diminished resources. By the 1870s lumbermen were seeking new reserves. They had two alternatives. They could either move west and compete with Californian-financed firms in the underdeveloped forests of the Pacific and Mountain regions, or they could go south to the Yellow Pine areas of the Gulf States. Few as yet thought about remaining in the Midwest to practise conservation [D. C. Smith, 1974].

Of these three areas the Lakes' region provides the clearest example of frontier exploitation. Here loggers frequently moved ahead of farmers, but they rarely remained isolated for long because they needed to sell in local markets. Soon partnerships and companies were formed, and thereafter whatever individualism remained lay with the lumberjacks whose exploits in felling trees or driving logs downriver tend to be romanticised versions of the monotonous and arduous tasks of manual workers. Certainly the technology and transportation of the mid-century were not sophisticated enough to have eliminated personal feats, but already there was considerable structural organisation [A. M. Larson, 1949; R. F. Fries, 1951; M. Walsh, 1972]. In lumbering a revisionist interpretation of frontier activity as a business venture can emerge before a heroic view has taken hold.

Two corollaries follow from the capitalistic viewpoint. In terms of the frontier as a process, lumbering provides no support for Turner's sequential pattern of growth (see p. 11 above). Throughout the Lakes' pineries small towns quickly emerged as sawmill centres and headquarters of lumber firms [R. F. Fries, 1951; M. Walsh, 1972]. Though this

Midwestern experience is not identical with the earlier Appalachian or later Far Western areas in terms of personnel, resources or technology, all demanded some degree of organisation and urban growth in the exploitation and processing of a bulky low-value commodity. On the negative side, lumbering brought enormous waste and destruction, not merely in logging, processing and marketing, but also through fires. The dangers and consequences of destruction and pollution have already tempered the approval of rapid growth [S. L. Udall, 1963; W. R. Jacobs, 1978]. Current concern for long-term national interests may suggest more negative assessments of the logging frontier.

OTHER SPEARHEADS OF THE FRONTIER

The cutting edges of frontier expansion were not restricted to the transient exploiters of non-agricultural resources. Other groups like explorers, missionaries, soldiers, land surveyors or even territorial administrators have been given the credit for challenging the wilderness [H. E. Bolton, 1917; F. P. Prucha, 1953; W. H. Goetzman, 1966]. Their primary functions, however, were diplomatic, religious or defensive, and while their presence indicated growth potential, their vanguard position is not likely to attract much attention from economic historians.

EARLY WESTERN CITIES

But the concept of spearhead has not yet been exhausted. Indeed its most controversial use has involved reshuffling Turner's ingredients so that 'The towns were the spearhead of the frontier. Planted far in advance of the line of settlement, they held the West for the approaching population' [R. C. Wade, 1959a]. Though many historians would question the ability of urban nucleii to flourish in the wilderness without a viable hinterland, most now accept the modified proposition that cities were an integral part of the early stages of westward expansion [J. C. Schnell and P. E. McLear, 1972; B. Luckingham, 1974]. Pioneers who sought opportunities in an urban rather than a rural environment, competed to build centres which could provide both local services and commercial links with other parts of the country. Many such towns were planned: some never progressed beyond the drawing board, while others prospered for a short time and then faded into insignificance. Several, however, grew rapidly and became major nucleii. There was certainly a vibrant urban frontier which was blustering in character [R. C. Wade, 1959 b; D. J. Boorstin, 1965; J. W. Reps, 1979].

Having firmly established the presence of early western towns, revisionist historians now seek to explain their origins and differential rates of growth. Various suggestions emerge both in the numerous studies of individual cities and in the more general overviews. The geographical advantages of site and situation usually involve location on a waterway or near natural resources: Louisville at the Falls of the Ohio River, Milwaukee on Lake Michigan, or the bay harbour of San Francisco with its inland route of the Sacramento River, illustrate the former, while Denver, Colorado, was built round precious minerals and Eau Claire, Wisconsin, round lumber [B. Still, 1941; R. Fries, 1951; R. C. Wade, 1959 a; R. W. Lotchin, 1974; G. Barth, 1975; E. K. Muller, 1976, 1977]. The influence of transport in the shape of railroads contributed to the rapid development of Chicago [B. L. Pierce, vol. 2, 1940]. Rails were also important as town builders west of the Missouri River where tracks were often laid ahead of settlement [R. C. Overton, 1941; L. H. Jenks, 1944; H. E. Briggs, 1950]. Trade is another influential ingredient. In the antebellum prairies, nucleii grew to supply commercial farmers with consumer goods and mercantile services and to process farm commodities for export [A. E. Fishlow, 1965; J. G. Clark, 1966; E. K. Muller, 1976]. Several points like Pittsburgh or St Louis were linked into a long-distance commerce with older cities anxious to participate in any emerging western business [R. C. Wade, 1959 a; J. E. Vance, 1970]. Thus far the explanations for frontier towns are similar to those for general urban growth.

Other variables have been introduced to explain deviations. Considerations of defence spread a picket-line of military posts across the frontier. The creation of new political units, at the state, territorial or even local county level, provided numerous opportunities for urban development. Religion was an effective force in Utah. Speculation, individual entrepreneurship or its collective form of community leadership often prompted construction [L. J. Arrington, 1958; D. J. Boorstin, 1965; R. G. Athearn, 1967; M. J. Rohrbough, 1978; J. W. Reps, 1979]. There is obviously ample scope for debate with respect to various facets or particular instances, but most historians have accepted the presence and importance of an urban West beyond the dimension suggested by Turner (see p. 11 and 18 above).

BANKING AND FINANCE

In converting Turner's rural West into a dynamic economy capable of rapid growth, financial and industrial institutions and processes have received little systematic attention. This lack of information stems partly from the continuing interest of western historians in land use, and partly from the propensity of economic historians to concentrate either on the Northeastern region or on later periods. Recent concern with inter-regional trade and development-economics has stimulated some research on banking and capital flows, internal commerce and particular industries, but both detailed and general studies of early western financial and manufacturing operations still remain unwritten [D. C. North, 1956, 1961; M. Walsh, 1975].

Turner did not ignore the necessity for financial transactions on the frontier, but he did seem to equate western expansion with easy money policies and irresponsible banking behaviour [F. J. Turner, 1893]. This view of frontier *naïveté* about monetary affairs gained a widespread acceptability so that stories of wild-cat banking, bank failures, states outlawing banks, contradictory requests for hard specie and paper money, and demands for an inflated currency supply, have variously contributed to the image of an anti-capitalist area [J. D. Hicks, 1931; C. H. Golembe, 1952; B. Hammond, 1957]. From this perspective financial agents and institutions appear as grasping middlemen taking unearned profits from the hardworking producer.

Revisionist historians have challenged this negative view by suggesting that western banking and attitudes to money should be examined in detail and then placed in perspective. There was variety in the attempts to find appropriate financial institutions; examples of wild-cat banking in Michigan or unsuccessful state banking in Kentucky and Illinois in the 1830s can be offset by illustrations of the successful banks of Ohio, Indiana and Missouri, or of sound alternatives when banking was forbidden. On a wider level, the prohibition of state banks in the 1840s and 1850s should be seen in the context of national party politics rather than of western ignorance [C. H. Golembe, 1952; E. A. Erickson, 1971; W. G. Shade, 1972; A. E. Smith, 1973]. Furthermore even the supposedly irrational attitudes to mortgage rates become comprehensible when put in the context of competing demands for investment capital, the structure of the banking system, and the extra risks of loaning to unknown or distant borrowers [A. G. Bogue, 1955; D. C. North, 1956; B. Hammond, 1957; R. Sylla, 1969; L. E. Davis, 1971].

This more discerning approach has been strengthened as macroeconomists have broadened the debate by discussing the technical problems of capital markets and the promotion of financial and economic development. Westerners might be uninformed, act rashly or take wrong decisions, on both a short and a long-term basis, but they were little different from bankers, investors or politicians in other parts of the United States – or indeed the world [P. Temin, 1969; H. Rockoff, 1975]. Americans generally operated in a new and uncertain field of monetary expansion and control, and whatever type of financial system was adopted, there would be hardships and mistakes. The difficulties of resolving recessions and depressions in the twentieth century have only strengthened a more detached assessment of frontier finance.

FRONTIER MANUFACTURING

A better understanding of capital transactions might follow from a knowledge of manufacturing activities, but the workings of the frontier business sector are still little understood. Research into individual industries or areas at specific times has been remarkably slim [E. A. Riley, 1911; J. D. Norris, 1964; N. L. Crockett, 1970; M. Walsh, 1972], though the quantitative study of regional trends may generate new interest in testable hypotheses [F. Bateman, J. D. Foust and T. J. Weiss, 1971; F. Bateman and T. J. Weiss, 1975]. Some suggestions about the nature of business activity in three newly settled areas may offer some guidelines.

Manufacturing on the trans-Appalachian frontier at the turn of the nineteenth century consisted mainly of processing natural resources and farm products, and making utensils for local use. Two indispensable features were the gristmill and the sawmill, frequently operated on a custom basis. Sometimes a blacksmith, wagonmaker or cabinetware-maker might operate a small shop. Other craftsmen like tailors, shoemakers and tanners might be itinerants or part-time farmers. Further simple industries like potash and maple syrup-making were viable only if markets were accessible. Pioneer manufacturing, like its farming counter-part, was limited in output and unsophisticated in character, communities remaining as self-sufficient as possible. Essential goods like salt, sugar, coffee and gunpowder, and some household articles were imported, but high freight charges prevented long-distance shipment of many com-modities [R. M. Tryon, 1971; N. A. McNall, 1952; J. Van Wagenen, Jr, 1953].

By mid-century western industry had both matured and become more specialised. In the Lake regions, household manufacturing declined as merchants sold goods from the East by water. Artisans like tinsmiths or tailors also felt the pinch of competition, but some remained in business through specialising in quality work. Alternatively they might turn to manufacturing ready-made goods if capital was available: heavy industries became economically viable as local demands for farm machinery, steam engines, mill and rail equipment increased. The most rapid progress, however, was made in processing farm products and timber. Flour, meat, leather, liquor and lumber became important exports and contributed to building up the infrastructure of an expanding economy [M. Walsh, 1975]. The Midwestern Frontier thus demonstrated a precocious manufacturing capacity which is not apparent in the Turnerian pattern of evolutionary development.

Moving further west into Kansas, Nebraska and the Dakotas in the 1870s and 1880s, pioneer industry superficially seems to resemble the Midwestern experience. Railroads transported manufactured goods into the region and the processed farm commodities out of the region. There was still some local demand for craft skills, but household manufacture had practically disappeared. The rise of big business in older parts of the country and the increased efficiency of transport brought national division of labour and economies of scale, however, so that processing industries, like meat packing or flour milling, might thrive, but often as branch plants of large firms, and farm machinery and other equipment could be imported at competitive prices. Western manufacturing here was still related to local resources, but like farming, its form and capacity was now closely dependent on trends in the national economy [C. B. Kuhlmann, 1929; W. T. Hutchinson, 1935; G. Porter and H. C. Livesay, 1971; M. Walsh, 1978].

CONCLUSIONS

A survey of the non-agrarian stages of frontier growth suggests that westward expansion in the nineteenth century did not follow an orderly Turnerian process. Some stages preceeded or followed land settlement, but others were omitted or occurred simultaneously with farming. This diversity of development was a result of both geographical and historical factors, the discrete location of natural resources dictating the presence of some activities, while the technological advances in transportation and machinery enabled new regions to become part of an interdependent economy and to produce for the national market. Thus Turner's march of civilisation needs to be rearranged frequently to fit different places at different times.

5 Peopling the New Land

THE movement of people to the American frontier as a geographical place proceeded at different rates and in different directions throughout the nineteenth century. Information on this migration is available at local, regional and national levels, both for specific points in time and for longer periods, but little effort has yet been made to weave together the various sources to provide either a general framework of analysis for ascertaining the dimensions of population growth or specific case studies for testing major propositions about western settlement.

ALTERNATIVE APPROACHES TO FRONTIER MIGRATION

Contemporary observers and traditional historians have written graphic narratives of settling the new country, and when portraying general patterns they tend to produce epic sagas of America's folk migration [C. Wittke, 1940]. More often, however, they focus on particular groups, usually immigrants from Europe, or on small areas like a county or a township. The resulting detailed and often emotional accounts contain some numerical evidence as well as numerous personal experiences, but generally, though of value to genealogists, they are too parochial for comparative work.

Social scientists, migration model builders and quantifiers regard American movement to the frontier as part of the general phenomena of geographical mobility which can be explained in identifiable and rational categories. They have developed theoretical frameworks to be tested by empirical data, which are presented statistically by a series of variables. Constructs such as kinship networks, intervening opportunities, turnover rates, indices of similarity and concentration ratios offer measurable ways of conceptualising the experience of newcomers to the West [H. Runblom and H. Norman (eds), 1976]. But the process of theorising and quantifying has raised problems as well as possibilities. In addition to the interminable debate on methodology, at the expense of carrying out research, the use of proxy variables as a substitute for historical evidence has created difficulties not only in specification and testing, but also in acceptability [*Historical Methods*, 1967-date; C. J. Erickson, 1975 a; R. W. Fogel, 1975].

Revisionist historians examining frontier demography have leaned towards, though they have not always carried out, systematic analyses. Concentrating on particular places, groups or years, they ask precise questions which are answered quantitatively when the evidence is robust, and as clearly as possible when the evidence is piecemeal or absent. In formulating their questions these 'new' historians draw both on theories, either Turnerian or demographic, and their own empirical knowledge. In seeking the answers they turn primarily to the manuscript schedules of the federal Census, which provide a massive data bank on a decennial basis – at least from 1850 onwards. They then examine other local records which might provide numerical information. Life histories, letters, diaries and newspapers further fill out analytical frameworks [M. Curti, *et al.*, 1959; M. Throne, 1959; W. L. Bowers, 1960; W. G. Robbins, 1970; D. J. Wishart, 1973].

The main hypotheses subjected to this systematic re-examination are traditional themes. Frontier migration is assumed to be a selective process composed primarily of young adults and single males. Native-born American pioneers are, for the most part, supposed to favour short-distance moves, while immigrants prefer to 'fill-in' behind, by purchasing land from mobile Americans. Then perhaps the most renowned proposition is the crucible idea that a composite American nationality emerged from the frontier experience [F. J. Turner, 1893; C. W. Thornthwaite, 1934; M. L. Hansen, 1940; J. Potter, 1965, 1969]. The diverse pieces of new research are still forthcoming and they need to be welded together before a reasonable reconstruction of frontier demography can be attempted.

THE POPULATION OF THE FRONTIER AS PLACE

Some appreciation of the numerical dimensions of westward expansion in what might conveniently be identified as the Turnerian century, 1790–1890, is essential before examining particular hypotheses. The frontier as the reception place for millions of settlers is not readily ident-ifiable, because while the federal Census Volumes and the Statistical Atlases have provided evidence of population growth and distribution at decennial intervals, the frontier and the West remain loosely defined. In

1790 the West consisted of all of the trans-Appalachian country, but such a large and developing area could scarcely be regarded as pioneer by 1890. The periodic alterations of boundaries has not resolved the identity problem because the omission of maturing western areas is frequently an administrative device to amalgamate neighbouring states into a new region. However, on a general level, the regional approach does provide an impressionistic survey of population growth (see Tables III and IV).

Table III

Population Growth in the West[1]
1790−1890 (in '000)

Year	United States	Total in Eastern States	Total in Western States	Percentage of US in West
1790	3,929	3,820	109	1.8
1800	5,308	4,922	386	7.3
1810	7,240	6,162	1,078	14.9
1820	9.638	7,420	2,218	23.0
1830	12,866	9,194	3,672	28.5
1840	17,069	10,692	6,377	37.4
1850	23,192	13,207	9,885	42.6
1860	31,443	15,958	15,485	49.2
1870	39,818	19,412	20,406	51.2
1880	50,156	22,105	28,051	55.9
1890	62,948	28,266	36,682	58.3

NOTES: (1) The West here is an approximation and is the equivalent of all regions except New England, the Middle Atlantic and the South Atlantic. It is thus *static* and is not synonymous with frontier in any of its definitions (two per square mile; the early years of settlement; the line between savagery and civilisation).

SOURCE: *Historical Statistics of The United States* (Washington, DC 1975).

The definition of frontier as place in terms of a population density of two persons per square mile has offered more scope for ascertaining the distribution of early settlement patterns. Tracing the receding frontier line through the maps of the Statistical Atlases, historians who follow this Turnerian approach find an irregular diminishing area [H. Gannett, 1898]. In 1790 most of the land west of the Appalachians was unsettled (see Map 4). But fifty years later only northern Michigan and northern Wisconsin qualified as frontier in the lands east of the Mississippi River (see Map 5). The 1840s and 1850s witnessed a noteworthy disruption of

Table IV

Regional Population Growth in the West, 1790–1890 (in '000)

Year	Total West	Great Lakes	(% of West)	North Central	(% of West)	South Central	(% of West)	Mountain	(% of West)	Pacific	(% of West)
1790	109	—		—		109	(100)	—		—	
1800	386	51	(13.2)	—		335	(86.8)	—		—	
1810	1,078	272	(25.2)	20	(1.9)	786	(72.9)	—		—	
1820	2,218	793	(35.8)	67	(3.0)	1,358	(61.2)	—		—	
1830	3,672	1,470	(40.0)	140	(3.8)	2,062	(56.2)	—		—	
1840	6,377	2,925	(45.9)	427	(6.7)	3,025	(47.4)	—		—	
1850	9,885	4,523	(45.8)	880	(8.9)	4,303	(43.5)	73	(0.7)	106	(1.1)
1860	15,485	6,927	(44.7)	2,170	(14.0)	5,769	(37.3)	175	(1.1)	444	(2.9)
1870	20,406	9,125	(44.7)	3,857	(18.9)	6,434	(31.5)	315	(1.6)	675	(3.3)
1880	28,051	11,207	(40.0)	6,157	(21.9)	8,919	(31.8)	653	(2.3)	1,115	(4.0)
1890	36,682	13,478	(36.7)	8,932	(24.3)	11,170	(30.5)	1,214	(3.3)	1,888	(5.2)

SOURCE: *Historical Statistics of the United States* (Wasington DC, 1975).

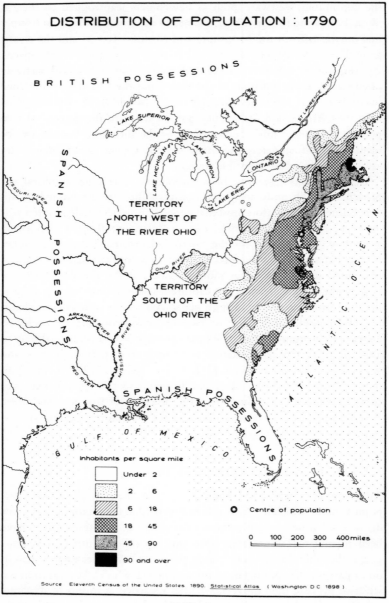

DISTRIBUTION OF POPULATION : 1790

BRITISH POSSESSIONS

LAKE SUPERIOR

ST. LAWRENCE RIVER

SPANISH POSSESSIONS

MISSOURI RIVER

LAKE MICHIGAN

LAKE HURON

L. ONTARIO

LAKE ERIE

TERRITORY
NORTH WEST OF
THE RIVER OHIO

OHIO RIVER

ARKANSAS RIVER

MISSISSIPPI RIVER

RED RIVER

TERRITORY
SOUTH OF THE
OHIO RIVER

ATLANTIC OCEAN

SPANISH POSSESSIONS

GULF OF MEXICO

Inhabitants per square mile

- Under 2
- 2 — 6
- 6 — 18
- 18 — 45
- 45 — 90
- 90 and over

○ Centre of population

0   100   200   300   400 miles

Source   Eleventh Census of the United States 1890. Statistical Atlas. (Washington D.C. 1898)

MAP 4

59

the continuous westward push as newcomers leapfrogged to the Far West. Following the Civil War, the steady extension of the main frontier line outwards from the Mississippi and Missouri Rivers and the erratic growth of scattered settlements further west, lessened the empty spaces. By 1890 many observers thought that the frontier line had virtually disappeared. Large portions of the Plains and the Mountains remained open, but these were of marginal utility (see Map 6). By using the Statistical Atlases and the county unit to measure the density of two persons per square mile the boundary of the shrinking frontier can be identified. Unfortunately the maps and the Census commentaries are rarely reproduced in accessible sources.

Demographers have not been satisfied with this geographical approach. Though uniformity and comparability are established in this way, some commentators insist that general numerical analysis at ten year intervals, though illuminating, cannot document frontier population accurately. Information for the interdecadal years, provided by other sources like state Censuses, directories, and random population counts, is of limited use for filling in more details, and the full dimensions of population change are thus not captured. Other commentators suggest that the density definition of two per square mile is so restrictive that it impedes consideration of most pioneer settlement, and they suggest increasing the figure to five or six per square mile and occasionally up to 18 if the area under consideration was empty at the previous Census and was still adjacent to open land [J. E. Eblen, 1965; J. E. Davis, 1977]. In these instances flexibility of definition seems to take precedence over comparability when encountering the diversity of frontier conditions. The dimensions of western demography therefore remain, at best imprecise, at worst contradictory.

AGE AND SEX STRUCTURE ON THE FRONTIER

Adopting an alternative definition of the frontier as an area the population of which has been officially recorded for no more than three decades, what new interpretations or revisions of traditional theses have been formulated? Numerous historians, including Turner, have suggested that there were more young people in a frontier region than in other parts of the country or in the nation as a whole. As migration is a selective process, then movers, whether regarded as misfits or dynamic members of society, are likely to be in the prime of their working life, between the ages of 20 and 40 [F. J. Turner, 1893; E. S. Lee, 1966; J. Potter, 1969; B. Thomas, 1973]. Most empirical studies of pioneer

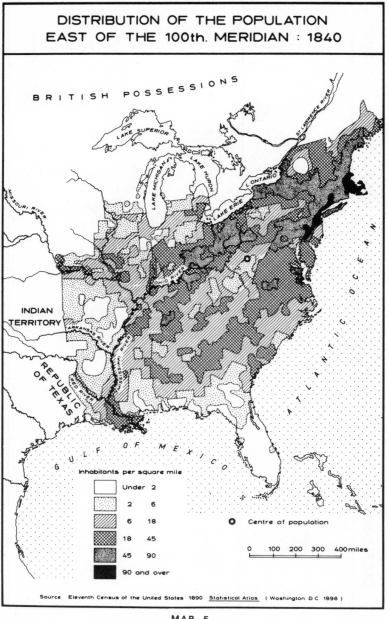

DISTRIBUTION OF THE POPULATION
EAST OF THE 100th. MERIDIAN : 1840

BRITISH POSSESSIONS

LAKE SUPERIOR

LAKE MICHIGAN

LAKE HURON

LAKE ERIE

L. ONTARIO

ST LAWRENCE RIVER

MISSOURI RIVER

OHIO RIVER

INDIAN TERRITORY

ARKANSAS RIVER

MISSISSIPPI RIVER

REPUBLIC OF TEXAS

RED RIVER

ATLANTIC OCEAN

GULF OF MEXICO

Inhabitants per square mile

Under 2
2 — 6
6 — 18
18 — 45
45 — 90
90 and over

⊙ Centre of population

0   100   200   300   400 miles

Source   Eleventh Census of the United States 1890   Statistical Atlas   (Washington D.C. 1898)

MAP 5

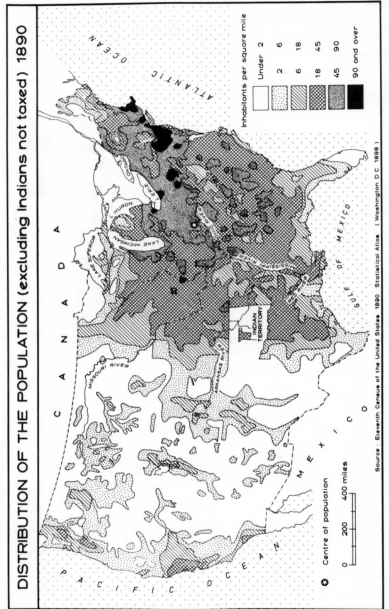

DISTRIBUTION OF THE POPULATION (excluding Indians not taxed) 1890

Inhabitants per square mile

Under 2
2 — 6
6 — 18
18 — 45
45 — 90
90 and over

CANADA

ATLANTIC OCEAN

PACIFIC OCEAN

GULF OF MEXICO

MEXICO

LAKE SUPERIOR
L. HURON
LAKE MICHIGAN
L. ONTARIO
L. ERIE

MISSOURI RIVER
ARKANSAS RIVER
MISSISSIPPI RIVER

INDIAN TERRITORY

⊛ Centre of population

0   200   400 miles

Source : Eleventh Census of the United States 1890 Statistical Atlas (Washington D.C. 1898)

MAP 6

communities confirm a youthful population focusing on this age-span.

Having made the general observation, the search for greater precision produces as many differences as similarities. In the average frontier agricultural county in the period 1840−60 there were more men in their twenties and thirties than in the United States as a whole. But there was the same proportion of women in their twenties and fewer women in their thirties than in the country at large [J. E. Eblen, 1965]. At an earlier period, 1800−40, frontier America was also young, but white migrants in the South were younger than their northern counterparts [J. E. Davis, 1977]. After the Civil War the age differentials between new farming frontiers and older parts of the nation narrowed as job opportunities expanded in the cities. If the geographically discrete mining or lumbering frontiers are analysed then the preponderance of young workers is much more noticeable than on the continuously moving farming frontier. But new urban dwellers displayed diversity even within the same region [R. C. Wade, 1959 a; R. Mann, 1972; K. N. Conzen, 1976]. Recent studies seem to add little rigour to the original proposition that the frontier was peopled by the relatively young.

What about the other familiar notion of frontier demography − namely that it was male-dominated? The economic opportunities of the new country presumably attracted men who were either single, or who left their wives and families behind temporarily. Certainly Turner failed to recognise the presence of women on the frontier, and most historians have followed suit, without considering that they were making some 40 per cent or more of the pioneers invisible. Census figures, however, clearly demonstrate a female participation in the westward movement (see Table V).

Certainly for most of the nineteenth century there were fewer women in various parts of the West than there were in older sections of the country, but again the generalisation masks different patterns. Wives often migrated to farms with their husbands, or joined them soon after, and single farmers were anxious to find female partners. Women were essential in running a viable enterprise when pioneers intended to remain in the new country. In the Far West, however, where mining was predominant, or in the lumbering regions of the Great Lakes, men noticeably outnumbered women, if only for short periods of time (see Table V). Yet even in mining communities there were more women than traditional sources have indicated. Doubtless researchers, having now established the academic respectability of the frontierswoman as a subject for study, will soon provide more evidence for modifying the male-dominated thesis [G. G. Riley, 1977; J. R. Jeffrey, 1979].

Table V

Males per 100 Females in the West

Year	United States	Middle West[1]	Mountain and Pacific West[2]
1790	103.7*		
1800	103.9*	117.4*	
1810	104.0*	111.9*	
1820	103.3	111.6	
1830	103.1	108.5	
1840	103.7	110.3	
1850	104.3	108.7	280.9
1860	104.7	108.9	214.2
1870	102.3	107.1	159.8
1880	103.6	108.0	153.3
1890	105.0	107.7	141.9

NOTES: (1) Used as an approximation of the Agrarian Frontier. (2) Used as an approximation of the Mining Frontier. * Whites only.

SOURCE: *Historical Statistics of the United States* (Washington DC, 1975).

FAMILIES ON THE FRONTIER

Many pioneers were married and had children. Thus migration — at least to agricultural and urban frontiers — was as much a family affair as a single person's prerogative. The nuclear household may not have been readily visible in mining and lumber camps, but it was the basic unit of social structure in most of the West [M. Curti, *et al.*, 1959; M. Throne, 1959; J. M. Faragher, 1979; J. R. Jeffrey, 1979; J. D. Unruh, Jr, 1979]. What then can be said about the size and composition of these families? If Turner or Malthus were correct, then frontier areas should witness higher fertility than elsewhere because they offered cheap land and abundant opportunity to people in the family-formation stage of life.

Current findings emerging from scattered studies of particular places at specific points in time, suggest that though family size and age of children varied within and between specified areas, frontier families were not markedly dissimilar to those elsewhere in the United States [M. Throne, 1959; J. Modell, 1971; J. R. Jeffreys, 1979]. Decisions on family size were subject to a variety of factors, including age at family formation, economic situation, personal beliefs, information on birth control and

64

degree of urbanisation [K. N. Conzen, 1976; D. Leet, 1976; M. A. Vinovskis, 1976; R. A. Easterlin, et al., 1978]. There was no clear-cut relationship between fertility and new settlement. By implication family values and standards were transmitted to the frontier and were not shaped by the environment. Further detailed studies comparing households in different parts of the country are, however, needed before any tentative, let alone definitive statements can be made, but analyses based on manuscript Census schedules suggest that frontier demography was more complex than Turner's march of young men.

MOBILITY ON THE FRONTIER

Were frontier settlers of whatever age, sex and family structure mobile? Obviously early population growth resulted primarily from westward migration. But did many pioneers move on through rather than to a given area? Did communities experience a high incidence of turnover, which contributed to making Americans a nation in motion? These questions are not new; nor indeed are some of the answers. However, the systematic tracing of individuals backwards and forwards over time and space has provided better estimates about the degree of mobility on the frontier. In turn this detailed research has revived the long-standing debate on types of mobility and reasons why pioneers located where they did.

Given the vast continental domain, it was perhaps natural that geographical mobility was commonly associated with the frontier. Traditional portrayals of the first wave of explorers, trappers and miners, supported the notion of rapid passage, and this view of the essentially transient nature of pioneers exploiting natural resources has been further substantiated by quantitative studies [G. N. Enberg, 1948; M. Curti, et al., 1959; R. Mann, 1972]. Settlements servicing the needs of miners or loggers might grow, but many of their early residents moved on when the minerals, lumber or fur-bearing animals were depleted.

Were farmers and town dwellers who might be expected to be more permanent residents also footloose? Analyses of the early decades of settlement in several parts of the Midwest point to a turnover of some 65 to 75 per cent among farm operators [J. C. Malin, 1935; M. Curti, et al., 1959; W. L. Bowers, 1960; P. J. Coleman, 1962 (repr. 1969)]. The mobility of agricultural labourers was even higher [W. L. Bowers, 1960; D. E. Schob, 1975]. Urban communities in the West were also unstable. Early Roseburg in Oregon, and Jacksonville in Illinois, had highly transient populations, while only a third of Houston's free residents of

1850 remained there a decade later. City directories point to similar or higher rates of movement in Milwaukee in the 1850s or Omaha in the 1880s [W. G. Robbins, 1970; H. P. Chudacoff, 1972; K. N. Conzen, 1976; D. H. Doyle, 1978; S. Jackson, 1978]. Restlessness was normal throughout the frontier.

It was not, however, a frontier prerogative. Movement to the burgeoning cities from the countryside, and from abroad, suggests that Turner's frontier and abundant land explanation must be expanded to embrace economic opportunity of a wider nature [F. A. Shannon, 1945; D. M. Potter, 1954; P. A. M. Taylor, 1971; G. W. Pierson, 1973]. Urban dwellers who moved between and within cities point to another residential fluidity, which in part may have become a habit [S. Thernstrom and P. R. Knights, 1970].

This increased awareness that Americans generally were very volatile in the nineteenth century has broadened the debate on frontier mobility. American historians have looked both to their foreign counterparts and to colleagues in other disciplines like geography, sociology and economics to see whether their approaches to migration flows can offer new insights. In the ensuing exchange, migration models have been developed, whereby a series of steps are built up, and the correct combination triggers off movement in a so-called value-added process. Historical sources can be used to measure new categories like intervening obstacles, structural strains or personal considerations as well as the more conventional push and pull factors [C. J. Erickson, 1975 b; H. Rumblom and H. Norman (eds), 1976]. Though greater precision and numeracy is now apparent in discussing migration to and within the West, much analytical work remains to be accomplished before any overall assessment can be made about frontier mobility.

WHY PIONEERS MOVED WEST

In the meanwhile economic opportunity retains the paramount place in most explanations of mobility, though there is considerable room for variation in this quest for material gain. Clearly many farmers, discouraged by poor crop outputs, marketing and other problems, moved to empty lands with a similar climate and vegetation, hoping to capitalise on their experience to get ahead [R. K. Vedder and L. E. Galloway, 1975)]. Some pioneers were speculators and bought lands further west, mainly to gain from their appreciation in value [R. P. Swierenga, 1977]. Others were influenced by propaganda and by special concessions like those offered by the transcontinental railroads

[R. C. Overton, 1941; H. E. Briggs, 1950; R. G. Athearn, 1971; A. Martin, 1976]. Still others sought their fortunes in the mineral resources of the Far West [R. W. Paul, 1947, 1963]. No migration wholly ignored economic considerations, and thus the frontier may still be considered as some form of direct or indirect safety-valve [E. Von Nardroff, 1962; J. K. Putnam, 1976] (see p.17 above).

But economic improvement alone will not explain all westward migration. The search for religious freedom, personified in the Mormon Trek to the Great Basin Kingdom, is perhaps the best known exception, though political refugees also went west [C. Wittke, 1940; H. S. Lucas, 1955; L. J. Arrington, 1958]. Family and ethnic ties appear to have strongly influenced some settlement, while the quest for improved health in a better climate explains some movement to the Far West [J. E. Baur, 1959; P. A. M. Taylor, 1971]. To what extent the love of adventure and the tradition of migration can be measured as powerful factors is a problem, but they are frequently listed in both literary and historical works.

ORIGINS OF THE FRONTIER POPULATION

This trait of restlessness frequently associated with Americans has contributed to another proposition about frontier demography, namely that immigrants acted as replacements, taking over lands vacated by the onward-moving American pioneer [M. L. Hansen, 1940]. Certainly studies of internal migration point to a regular stepwise pattern originating largely from states that were settled some 40 or 50 years earlier [C. W. Thornthwaite, 1934; F. A. Shannon, 1945; B. E. Lathrop, 1949], but not all frontier residents were born in the United States. Census records and land entries demonstrate that immigrants farmed virgin soil on both sides of the Mississippi River, and they also took an active part in developing new towns [R. C. Overton, 1941; M. Curti, et al., 1959; P. A. M. Taylor, 1971; R. W. Lotchin, 1974; K. N. Conzen, 1976; D. H. Doyle, 1978]. Nor were they remarkably less mobile than their numerous American-born counterparts: the presence of ethnic groups may suggest higher persistence levels, but detailed studies do not uphold the notion of two noticeably different patterns of restlessness [M. Curti et al., 1959; J. C. Hudson, 1976; F. C. Luebke, 1977; D. A. McQuillan, 1979].

Do these similarities suggest that all newcomers to the West were alike? Turner certainly implied that immigrants were merged into some composite American nationality by a frontier melting process. But he

67

was not very precise about the mechanics of ethnic and racial integration. Presumably the common experience of adjusting to a new physical environment and to a fluid society required widespread participation, which in turn meant that particular foreign traits were short-lived [S. Elkins and E. McKitrick, 1954]. These were fused in the 'frontier crucible'.

However, the traditional melting-pot thesis, which belongs neither exclusively to Turner, nor to the frontier, has been discredited in a nation anxious to promote a multinational appearance. Ethnic and racial status is now an asset and different groups are encouraged to retain their cultural values and their language provided that some overtures are made towards Americanisation. A thesis of modified cultural pluralism which incorporates spatial congregation with economic, social and political participation is currently being used to analyse both rural enclaves and urban ghettoes [K. N. Conzen, 1976; J. C. Hudson, 1976; F. C. Luebke, 1977; D. A. McQuillan, 1979]. Newcomers may adjust painlessly or otherwise to better living standards in the United States, but they postpone full assimilation.

If, then, the frontier was settled by groups who retained their cultural identity, what can be said about their origin and their adjustments to the new country? Abundant information is available in local studies about white native-born American pioneers who were numerically dominant and who have traditionally been regarded as some homogeneous ideal. Their migration flows and settlement patterns can certainly be documented from state of birth data recorded in the manuscript Census and from personal reminiscences [C. W. Thornthwaite, 1934; B. E. Lathrop, 1949]. But regional differences between Yankees who swept across the Old Northwest, Southerners who relocated in the Gulf areas or Midwesterners who moved either to Oregon or on to the western prairies can also be enumerated. These in turn point to differences of opinion on, for example, slavery and political affiliation, and to cultural variety in architectural styles and community associations [P. Kleppner, 1970; A. E. Smith, 1973]. Heterogeneity among pioneers born in different parts of the United States is perceptible, but many new monographs are required to modify some of the sweeping generalisations concerning the so-called normal American pattern of behaviour on the frontier.

The immigrant presence in the West is also recorded in numerous volumes. But the ethnic contribution is more difficult to place in a satisfactory framework because of the nature of immigrant history and its patchy coverage. Most studies trace specific national groups from their homeland to their destinations in the New World, and then through their various phases of adjustment [H. S. Lucas, 1955; K. Hvidt, 1975; I. Semmingsen, 1978]. But the frontier experience forms only a small part of this process, even for the well-known groups like Scandinavians and Germans who were particularly attracted to the land. Immigrant frontier analysis is thus problematic.

Some progress is visible in the new studies of rural and urban frontiers which use the common data base of the manuscript schedules of the federal Census from 1850 onwards. These trace migration routes and residential patterns and also construct variables measuring participation, inter-ethnic marriage, upward mobility and other categories now used in discussing assimilation [H. P. Chudacoff, 1972; C. Stephenson, 1974; D. H. Doyle, 1978]. Other sources, like land-record entries, city directories, poll books and newspapers, provide additional materials for collective biographies of previously anonymous settlers [K. N. Conzen, 1976; J. C. Hudson, 1976]. In this way new dimensions are given to the more conventional narratives of the major immigrant groups.

Further dimensions are added to the reconstruction of the ethnic experience on the frontier by including different foreign-born settlers. Immigrants from north-western Europe, who moved west from the 1840s onwards, have previously dominated general discussions of pioneering by aliens. Other groups from central and south-eastern Europe, or from Asia and the other Americas, have received comparatively little attention. Certainly many immigrants from countries like Greece, Italy or Russia arrived in the late nineteenth or early twentieth centuries when good new land was scarce and there were more job opportunities in the cities. They are less visible, but they are not absent from the rural west. Quantitative evidence, aided by limited descriptive information, now offers insights on less well-known groups like Poles, Czechs or French Canadians [F. C. Luebke, 1977; D. A. McQuillan, 1979]. West Coast immigrants who moved east also suggest a different frontier complexion [G. P. Barth, 1964].

Still another strand — the non-white, native-born Americans, namely Indians, Blacks and Mexicans — must be added to complete any revised population profile of the frontier. The Indians suffered enforced mobility as they were pushed first west and then on to smaller and smaller reservations [W. T. Hagan, 1961; W. E. Washburn, 1975]. Blacks in bondage moved west as farm labourers. As free persons they took up diverse occupations, but relatively few seem to have migrated to the frontier [E. D. Genovese, 1965; W. S. Savage, 1976; K. W. Porter 1971]. Mexican Americans, for the most part, remained in the Southwest as an unskilled labour force either for rich Spanish landowners or for acquisitive Anglo-Americans [D. J. Weber, 1973]. Grouped together these minorities point to a multiracial society of sorts, but one in which opportunity was not as readily available as some historians have portrayed. Discussion of frontier populations has yet to be correctly balanced.

CONCLUSIONS

It is very difficult to make any viable general statements about the peopling of the new country. Perhaps a comprehensive study may never be written because of the temporal and spatial diversity of the frontier in the nineteenth century and the variety of source materials and styles of approach. Regional analyses focusing on limited time-periods may provide the most incisive insights, but these will need to incorporate both numerical data and the findings of other cross-sectional approaches like family, women's, Indian or immigrant histories. There is still ample scope for detailed research and then for general interpretations.

6 Conclusions and Suggestions

THE American frontier has become academically unfashionable in recent years both as a subject in its own right and as an integral part of the broader study of the United States. This tendency notwithstanding, a knowledge of the acquisition, disposal, settlement and growth of the lands west of the Appalachians in the late eighteenth and nineteenth centuries is essential to appreciate the scale, rate and significance of the economic development of the country. In acquiring this information the Turner thesis is a central argument which most specialised research and general writing has acknowledged, whether by way of acceptance, dismissal or partial agreement.

Though written some ninety years ago the Frontier Thesis has survived the test of time, not only for American history, but also for the study of newly settled lands throughout the world [M. W. Mikesell, 1960; M. T. Katzman, 1975; W. T. Jackson, 1976; A. Hennessey, 1978]. The hypothesis has been in and out of vogue, and has been buried and revived several times, either in accordance with the socio-economic conditions of the day, or as new evidence and methodologies add some different facets or suggest alternative approaches. Currently it appears dated because models of development economics focus on urban-industrial growth, and also because the problems of scarce resources are not compatible with the abundance and wastefulness of previous generations. Furthermore, computer-minded scholars insist that theories should be specified precisely and subject to rigorous testing with quantitative evidence.

But both the Turnerian disciples and critics have and still are demanding too much of the thesis or even of Turner's later statements. 'The Significance of the American Frontier' was never meant to be a definitive piece of work: it was essentially a speculative essay posing questions which readers should try to answer by undertaking specific research. If the framework is used as a series of suggestions, then the central issues about the West and its relationship to the United States are certainly raised. Turner wished to ascertain what was the impact of abundant resources in general, and of free land in particular. How was the frontier developed, when, by whom and at what rate? What impact did the new regions have on the older parts of the country? Indeed Turner's fame rests on the fact that he asked all the interesting questions about frontier development.

It does not seem likely, at the moment, that any new questions are going to be formulated. There are new ways of answering the old questions and the answers may not coincide, but fresh evidence and modern research techniques do not automatically require or even imply the creation of new hypotheses when old ones are flexible. What they do demand is an ongoing revision which attempts to place the results in some useful and general perspective.

Select Bibliography

The following list is highly selective and I apologise to the many authors of other works which have both directly and indirectly influenced the shape and content of this pamphlet. For further bibliographical references see Billington, R. A., *Westward Expansion. A History of the American Frontier*, 4th ed. (New York, 1974) and Paul, R. W. and Etulain, R. W. (eds), *The Frontier and the American West* (Arlington Heights, Illinois, 1977). The most convenient source of statistics is *The Historical Statistics of the United States. Colonial Times to 1970*, 2 vols (Washington, DC, 1975). The most useful atlas is Gannett, H., *The Statistical Atlas of the United States. Eleventh Census* (Washington, DC, 1898), but this is a rare volume. A more accessible alternative is Paullin, C. O., *Atlas of the Historical Geography of the United States* (Washington, DC, 1932).

None of the standard texts are specifically designed for an audience of economic and social historians, but they all contain pertinent information. The best known textbook is Billington, R. A., *Westward Expansion. A History of the American Frontier*, 4th ed. (New York, 1974). Three recent textbooks suggest other approaches and insights: Bartlett, R. A., *The New Country. A Social History of the American Frontier, 1776–1890* (New York, 1974); Gibson, A. M., *The West in the Life of the Nation* (Lexington, Mass., 1976) and Merk, F., *History of the Westward Movement* (New York, 1978).

Several anthologies bring together some central articles and some incisive commentary by compilers. They include Bogue, A. G., Phillips, T. D. and Wright, J. E. (eds), *The West of the American People* (Itasca, Illinois 1970); Clark, J. G. (ed.), *The Frontier Challenge. Responses to the Trans-Mississippi West* (Lawrence, Kansas, 1971); Ellis, D. M. (ed.), *The Frontier in American Development: Essays in Honor of Paul Wallace Gates* (Ithaca, New York, 1969); Fogel, R. W. and Engerman, S. L. (eds), *The Reinterpretation of American Economic History* (New York, 1971); Klingaman, D. C. and Vedder, R. K. (eds), *Essays in Nineteenth Century Economic History. The Old Northwest* (Athens, Ohio, 1975); McDermott, J. F. (ed.), *The Frontier Re-Examined* (Urbana, Illinois, 1967); Scheiber,

H. N. (ed.), *The Old Northwest. Studies in Regional History, 1787–1910* (Lincoln, Nebraska, 1969).

The following abbreviations have been used for these journals.

AH	*Agricultural History*
AHR	*American Historical Review*
JAH	*Journal of American History*
JEH	*Journal of Economic History*
MVHR	*Mississippi Valley Historical Review*
WHQ	*Western Historical Quarterly*

Abott, C., 'The Plank Road Enthusiasm in the Antebellum Middle West', *Indiana Magazine of History*, LXVII (1971).

Allen, H. C., 'F. J. Turner and the Frontier in American History', in Allen H. C. and Hill, C. P. (eds), *British Essays in American History* (London, 1957).

Arrington, L. J., *Great Basin Kingdom. An Economic History of the Latter Day Saints, 1830–1890* (Cambridge, Mass., 1958).

Athearn, R. G., *Forts of the Upper Missouri* (Englewood Cliffs, New Jersey, 1967).

——, *Union Pacific Country* (Chicago, 1971).

Atherton, L., *The Cattle Kings* (Bloomington, Indiana, 1961).

Barth, G. P., *Bitter Strength. A History of the Chinese in the United States, 1850–1870* (Cambridge, Mass., 1964).

——, *Instant Cities: Urbanization and the Rise of San Francisco and Denver* (New York, 1975).

Bateman, F., Foust, J. D. and Weiss, T. J., 'Large-Scale Manufacturing in the South and West, 1850–1860', *Business History Review*, XLV (1971).

Bateman, F. and Weiss, T. J., 'Comparative Regional Development in Antebellum Manufacturing', *JEH*, XXXV (1975).

Baur, J. E., 'The Health Seekers in the Westward Movement, 1830–1890', *MVHR*, XLVI (1959).

Benson, L., 'The Historical Background to Turner's Frontier Essay', *AH*, XXV (1951).

Berkhofer, R. F. Jr, 'Space, Time, Culture and the New Frontier', *AH*, XXXVIII (1964).

Berry, T. S., 'Gold! but how much?' *California Historical Quarterly*, LV (1976).

Bidwell, P. W and Falconer, J. I., *History of Agriculture in the Northern United States, 1620–1860* (Washington DC, 1925).

Billington, R. A. *America's Frontier Heritage* (New York, 1963).

——, *Frederick Jackson Turner. Historian, Scholar, Teacher* (New York, 1973).

——, *The Frontier Thesis. Valid Interpretation of American History* (New York, 1966).

——, *The Genesis of the Frontier Thesis. A Study in Historical Creativity* (San Marino, California, 1971).

Blackburn, G. and Richards, S. L. Jr, 'A Demographic History of the West: Manistee County, Michigan, 1860', *JAH*, LVII (1970).

Bogue, A. G., *From Prairie to Cornbelt. Farming on the Illinois and Iowa Prairies in the Nineteenth Century* (Chicago, 1963).

——, *Money at Interest. The Farm Mortgage on the Middle Border* (Ithaca, New York, 1955).

——, 'Land Credit for Northern Farmers', *AH*, L (1976).

Bogue, A. G. and Bogue, M. B., 'Profits and the Frontier Land Speculator', reprinted in Fogel, R. W. and Engerman, S. L. (eds), *The Reinterpretation of American Economic History* (New York, 1971).

Bolton, H. E., 'The Mission as a Frontier Institution in the Spanish American Colonies', *AHR*, XXXIII (1917).

Boorstin, D. J., *The Americans. The National Experience* (New York, 1965).

Bowen, W. A., *Willamette Valley. Migration and Settlement on the Oregon Frontier* (Seattle, 1978).

Bowers, W. L., 'Crawford Township, 1850–1870. A Population Study of a Pioneer Community', *Iowa Journal of History*, LVIII (1960).

Briggs, H. E., *Frontiers of the Northwest. A History of the Upper Missouri Valley*, repr. ed. (New York, 1950).

Chudacoff, H. P., *Mobile Americans. Residential and Social Mobility in Omaha, 1880–1920* (New York, 1972).

Clark, J. G., *The Grain Trade of the Old Northwest* (Urbana, Illinois, 1966).

Clayton, J. L., 'The Growth and Economic Significance of the American Fur Trade, 1790–1890', *Minnesota History*, XL (1966).

Clelland, R. G., *Cattle On A Thousand Hills*, 2nd ed. (San Marino, California, 1951).

Cochran, T. C., 'The Paradox of American Economic Growth', *JAH*, LXI (1975).

Coleman, P. J., 'Restless Grant County: Americans on the Move', in Scheiber, H. N. (ed.), *The Old Northwest* (Lincoln, Nebraska, 1969).

Connor, S. V. and Skaggs, J. M., *Broadcloth and Britches. The Santa Fe Trade* (College Station, Texas, 1977).

Conzen, K. N., *Immigrant Milwaukee, 1836–60. Accommodation and Community in a Frontier City* (Cambridge, Mass., 1976).

Crockett, N. L., *The Woollen Industry of the Midwest* (Lexington, Kentucky, 1970).

Curti, M. *et al., The Making of an American Community. A Case Study of Democracy in a Frontier County* (Stanford, 1959).

Dale, E. E., *The Range Cattle Industry*, new ed. (Norman, Oklahoma, 1960).

Danhof, C. H., *Change in Agriculture. The Northern United States, 1820–1870* (Cambridge, Mass., 1969).

David, P. A., 'The Mechanization of Reaping in the Ante-Bellum Midwest', in Fogel, R. W. and Engerman, S. L. (eds), *The Reinterpretation of American Economic History* (New York, 1971).

Davis, J. E., *Frontier America 1800–1840. A Comparative Demographic Analysis of the Frontier Process* (Glendale, California, 1977).

Davis, L. E., 'Capital Mobility and American Growth', in Fogel, R. W. and Engerman, S. L. (eds), *The Reinterpretation of American Economic History* (New York, 1971).

Dennen, R. T., 'Some Efficiency Effects of Nineteenth Century Federal Land Policy. A Dynamic Analysis', *AH*, LI (1977).

Dick, E., *Conquering The Great American Desert: Nebraska* (Lincoln, Nebraska, 1975).

Dobyns, H. F., *Native American Historical Demography. A Critical Bibliography* (Bloomington, Indiana, 1976).

——, 'Estimating Aboriginal American Population. An Appraisal of Techniques with a New Hemisphere Estimate', *Current Anthropology*, VII (1966).

Doyle, D. H., *The Social Order of a Frontier Community. Jacksonville, Illinois, 1825–70* (Urbana, Illinois, 1978).

Drache, H. M., *The Day of the Bonanza: A History of Bonanza Farming in the Red River Valley of the North* (Fargo, North Dakota, 1964).

Easterlin, R. A., Alter, G. and Condran, G. A., 'Farms, and Farm Families in Old and New Areas; The Northern States in 1860', in Hareven, T. K. and Vinovskis, M. A. (eds), *Family and Population in Nineteenth Century America* (Princeton, 1978).

Eblen, J. E., *The First and Second American Empires. Governors and Territorial Government, 1784–1912* (Pittsburg, 1968).

——, 'An Analysis of Nineteenth Century Frontier Populations', *Demography*, II (1965).

Elkins, S. and McKitrick, E., 'A Meaning for Turner's Frontier', *Political Science Quarterly*, LXIX (1954).

Enberg, G. B., 'Who were the Lumberjacks?', in Scheiber, H. N. (ed.), *The Old Northwest* (Lincoln, 1969).

Engerman, S. L., 'Some Economic Issues Relating to Railroad Subsidies and the Evaluation of Land Grants', *JEH*, XXXII (1972).

Erickson, C. J., 'Quantative History', *AHR*, LXXX (1975, a).

——, 'Explanatory Models in Immigration and Migration Research', Unpublished Paper (Conference on Scandinavian Emigration to the United States, Oslo, 1975, b).

Erickson, E. A., *Banking in Frontier Iowa, 1836–1865* (Ames, Iowa, 1971).

Faragher, J. M., *Women and Men on the Overland Trail* (New Haven, 1979).

Fishlow, A. E., *American Railroads and the Transformation of the Ante-Bellum Economy* (Cambridge, Mass., 1965).

Fite, G. C., *The Farmer's Frontier, 1865–1900* (New York, 1966).

Fogel, R. W., 'The Limits of Quantitative Methods in History', *AHR*, LXXX (1975).

Fogel, R. W. and Rutner, J. L., 'The Efficiency Effects of Federal Land Policy, 1850–1900: A Report of Some Provisional Findings', in Aydelotte, W. O., Bogue, A. G. and Fogel, R. W. (eds), *The Dimensions of Quantitative Research in History* (Princeton, 1972).

Fries, R. F., *Empire in Pine. Lumbering in Wisconsin, 1830–1900* (Madison, Wisconsin, 1951).

Gates, P. W., *California Ranchos and Farms, 1846–1862* (Madison, Wisconsin, 1967).

——, *History of Public Land Law Development* (Washington, DC, 1968).

——, *Landlords and Tenants on the Prairie Frontier. Studies in American Land Policy* (Ithaca, New York, 1973).

——, *The Farmer's Age: Agriculture, 1815–1860* (New York, 1960).

——, 'An Overview of American Land Policy', *AH*, L (1976).

Genovese, E. D., *The Political Economy of Slavery* (New York, 1965).

Goetzman, W. H., *Exploration and Empire. The Explorer and the Scientist in the Winning of the American West, 1805–1900* (New York, 1966).

——, 'The Mountain Men. The Brief and Glorious Era of the Frontier Trapper', *The American West*, XV (1978).

Golembe, C. H., *State Banks and the Economic Development of the West. 1830–1844* (New York, 1952).

Graebner, N. A. (ed.) *Manifest Destiny* (Indianapolis, 1968).

Gray, L. C., *History of Agriculture in the Southern United States to 1860*, 2 vols (Washington, D C, 1933).

Greever, W. S., *The Bonanza West. The Story of the Western Mining Rushes, 1848–1900* (Norman Oklahoma, 1963).

Gressley, G. M., *Bankers and Cattlemen* (New York, 1966).

——, 'The Turner Thesis: A Problem in Historiography', *AH*, XXXII (1958).

Hagan, W. T., *American Indians* (Chicago, 1961).

Hammond, B., *Banks and Politics in America from the Revolution to the Civil War* (Princeton, 1957).

Hansen, M. L., *The Immigrant in American History* (Cambridge, Mass., 1940).

Hawgood, J. A., *The American West* (London, 1967).

Henlein, P. C., *Cattle Kingdom in the Ohio Valley, 1783–1860* (Lexington, Kentucky, 1959).

Hennessey, A., *The Frontier in Latin American History* (London, 1978).

Hibbard, B. H., *A History of the Public Land Policies*, repr. ed. (Madison, Wisconsin, 1965).

Hicks, J. D., *The Populist Revolt: A History of the Farmers' Alliance and the People's Party* (Minneapolis, 1931).

Hofstadter, R., *The Age of Reform. From Bryan to F.D.R.* (New York, 1955).

——, *The Progressive Historians. Turner, Beard and Parrington* (New York, 1968).

Hornbeck, D., 'Mexican-American Land Tenure Conflict in California', *Journal of Geography*, LXXIV (1976).

Horsman, R., *The Frontier in the Formative Years, 1783–1815* (New York, 1970).

Hudson, J. C., 'Migration to an American Frontier', *Annals of the Association of American Geographers*, LXI (1976).

Hutchinson, W. T., *Cyrus Hall McCormick*, 2 vols (New York, 1935).

Hvidt, K., *Flight to America. The Social Background of 300,000 Danish Emigrants* (New York, 1975).

Jackson, S., 'Movin On'. Mobility Through Houston in the 1850's, *Southwestern Historical Quarterly*, LXXXI (1978).

Jackson, W. T., 'Australians and the Comparative Frontier', in Philp, K. R. and West, E. (eds), *The Walter Prescott Webb Memorial Lectures* (Austin, Texas, 1976).

Jacobs, W. R., *The Historical World of Frederick Jackson Turner* (New Haven, 1968).

——, 'Frontiersmen, Fur Traders and Other Varmints, An Ecological Appraisal of the Frontier in American History', American Historical Association, *Newsletter*, VIII (1970).

——, 'The Great Despoliation: Environmental Themes in American Frontier History', *Pacific Historical Review*, XLVII (1978).

Jeffrey, J. R., *Frontier Women: The Trans-Mississippi West 1840–1880* (New York, 1979),

Jenks, L. H., 'Railroads as an Economic Force in American Development', *JEH*, IV (1944).

Katzman, M. T., 'The Brazilian Frontier in Comparative Perspective', *Comparative Studies in Society and History*, XVII (1975).

Kleppner, P., *The Cross of Culture: Social Analysis of Midwestern Politics, 1850–1900* (New York, 1970).

Kuhlmann, C. B., *The Development of the Flour Milling Industry in the United States* (Boston, 1929).

Lamar, H. R., *The Trader on the American Frontier: Myth's Victim* (College Station, Texas, 1977).

——, 'Frederick Jackson Turner', in Cunliffe, M. and Winks, R. W. (eds), *Pastmasters. Some Essays on American Historians* (New York, 1969).

——, 'Persistent Frontier: The West in the Twentieth Century', *WHQ*, IV (1973).

Larson, A. M., *History of the White Pine Industry in Minnesota* (Minneapolis, 1949).

Lathrop, B. F., *Migration into East Texas, 1835–1860. A Study from the United States Census* (Austin, 1949).

Le Duc, T., 'History and Appraisal of U. S. Land Policy to 1862', in Ottoson, H. W. (ed.), *Land Use Policy and Problems in the United States* (Lincoln, Nebraska, 1963, a).

——, 'Public Policy, Private Investment and Land Use in American Agriculture, 1825–75', *AH*, XXXVII (1963, b).

Lee, E. S., 'A Theory of Migration', *Demography*, III, (1966).

Leet, D., 'The Determinants of Fertility Transition in Antebellum Ohio', *JEH*, XXXVI (1976).

Linden, F., 'Economic Democracy in the Slave South: An Appriasal of Some Recent Views', *Journal of Negro History*, XXXI (1946).

Loehr, R. C., 'Self Sufficiency on the Farm', *AH*, XXIV (1952).

Lotchin, R. W., *San Francisco, 1846–1856; From Hamlet to City* (New York, 1974).

Lucas, H. S., *Netherlanders in America. Dutch Immigration to the United States and Canada 1789–1950* (Ann Arbor, 1955).

Luckingham, B., 'The City in the Westward Movement – A Bibliographical Note', *WHQ*, V (1974).

Luebke, F. C., 'Ethnic Group Settlement on the Great Plains', *WHQ*, VIII (1977).

Lurie, J., 'Speculation, Risk and Profits. The Ambivalent Agrarian in the Late Nineteenth Century', *AH*, XLVI (1972).

Lurie, N. O., 'The Indian Claims Commission', American Academy of Political and Social Science, *Annals*, CCCCXXXVI (1978).

McNall, N. A., *An Agricultural History of the Genessee Valley, 1790–1860* (Philadelphia, 1952).

McQuillan, D. A., 'The Mobility of Immigrants and Americans: A Comparison of Farmers on the Kansas Frontier', *AH*, LIII (1979).

Mak, J., Haites, E. F. and Walton, G. M., *Western Transportation. The Era of Early Internal Development, 1810–1860* (Baltimore, 1975).

Malin, J. C., 'The Turnover of Farm Population in Kansas', *Kansas Historical Quarterly*, IV (1935).

——, 'The Adaptation of the Agricultural System to the Sub Humid Environment', *AH*, X (1936).

Mann, R., 'The Decade After the Gold Rush: Social Structure in Grass Valley and Nevada City, California, 1850–1860', *Pacific Historical Review*, XLI (1972).

Martin, A., *James J. Hill and the Opening of the Northwest* (New York, 1976).

Mayhew, A., 'A Reappraisal of the Causes of Farm Discontent, 1870–1900', *JEH*, XXXII (1972).

Meinig, D. W., *The Great Columbia Plain. A Historical Geography 1805–1910* (Seattle, 1968).

Meister, C. A., 'Demographic Consequences of Euro-American Contact on Selected American Indian Populations and Their Relationship to the Demographic Transition', *Ethnohistory*, XXIII (1976).

Merk, F., *Manifest Destiny and Mission in American History* (New York, 1963).

Mikesell, M. W., 'Comparative Studies in Frontier History', *Annals of the Association of American Geographers*, L (1960).

Mitchell, R. D., *Commercialism and Frontier. Perspectives on the Early Shenandoah Valley* (Charlottesville, Virginia, 1977).

Modell, J., 'Family Fertility on the Indiana Frontier', *American Quarterly*, XXIII (1971).

Muller, E. K., 'Selective Urban Growth in the Middle Ohio Valley, 1800–1860', *Geographical Review*, LXVI (1976).

——, 'Regional Urbanization and the Selective Growth of Towns in North American Regions', *Journal of Historical Geography*, III (1977).

Nash, R., 'The American Conservation Movement'. *Forum Press Series* (St Charles, Missouri, 1974).

Nichols, D. A., 'Civilization over Savage. Frederick Jackson Turner and the Indian', *South Dakota History*, II (1972).

Norris, J. D., *Frontier Iron: The Maramec Iron Works, 1826–1876* (Madison, Wisconsin, 1964).

North, D. C., *Growth and Welfare in the American Past. A New Economic History* (Englewood Cliffs, New Jersey, 1966).

——, *The Economic Growth of the United States 1790–1860* (New York, 1961).

——, 'International Capital Flows and the Development of the American West', *JEH*, XVI (1956).

Oglesby, R. E., 'The Fur Trade As Business', in McDermott, J. F. (ed.), *The Frontier Re-Examined* (Urbana, Illinois, 1967).

Oliphant, J. O., *On The Cattle Ranges of the Oregon Country* (Seattle, 1968).

Olmstead, A. L., 'The Mechanization of Reaping and Mowing in American Agriculture, 1833–1870', *JEH*, XXXV (1975).

Overton, R. C., *Burlington West. A Colonization History of the Burlington Railroad* (Cambridge, Mass., 1941).

Owsley, F. L., *Plain Folk of the Old South* (Baton Rouge, Louisiana, 1949).

Parker, W. N. (ed.), *The Structure of the Cotton Economy of the Antebellum South* (Washington, DC, 1970).

——, 'Productivity Growth in American Grain Farming: An Analysis of its Nineteenth Century Sources', in Fogel, R. W. and Engerman, S. L. (eds), *The Reinterpretation of American Economic History* (New York, 1971).

Paul, R. W., *California Gold. The Beginning of Mining in the Far West* (Cambridge, Mass., 1947).

——, *Mining Frontiers of the Far West, 1848–1880* (New York, 1963).

——, 'The Beginnings of Agriculture in California: Innovation vs Continuity', *California Historical Quarterly*, LII (1973).

Pierce, B. L., *A History of Chicago. (vol. 2) From Town to City, 1848–1871* (Chicago, 1940).

Pierson, G. W., *The Moving American* (New York, 1973).

Pomeroy, E., *The Pacific Slope. A History* (New York, 1965).

Porter, G. and Livesay, H. C., *Merchants and Manufacturers. Studies in the Changing Structure of Nineteenth-Century Marketing* (John Hopkins, 1971).

Porter, K. W., *The Negro on the American Frontier* (New York, 1971).

Potter, D. M., *People of Plenty. Economic Abundance and the American Character* (Chicago, 1954).

Potter, J., 'Some British Reflections on Turner and the Frontier', *Wisconsin Magazine of History*, LIII (1969).

——, 'The Growth of Population in America 1700–1860', in Glass, D. V. and Eversley, D.E.C. (eds), *Population in History. Essays in Historical Demography* (Chicago, 1965).

Prucha, F. P., *A Bibliographical Guide to the History of Indian-White Relations in the United States* (Chicago, 1977).

——, *Broadax and Bayonet. The Role of the United States Army in the Development of the Northwest, 1815—1860* (Madison, Wisconsin, 1953).

——, 'Books on American Indian Policy. A Half Decade of Important Work', *JAH* LXIII (1976).

Putnam, J. K., 'The Turner Thesis and the Westward Movement: A Reappraisal', *WHQ*, VII (1976).

Rastatter, E. H., 'Nineteenth Century Public Land Policy. The Case for the Speculator', in Klingaman, D. C. and Vedder, R. K. (eds), *Essays in Nineteenth Century Economic History. The Old Northwest* (Athens, Ohio, 1975).

Reps, J. W., *Cities of the American West: A History of Frontier Urban Planning* (Princeton, 1979).

Riley, E. A., *The Industrial Development of Chicago and Vicinity prior to 1880* (Chicago, 1911).

Riley, G. G., 'Women On The American Frontier', *Forum Press Series* (St Louis, Missouri, 1977).

Rittenhouse, J. D., *The Santa Fe Trail. A Historical Bibliography* (Albuquerque, New Mexico, 1971).

Robbins, R. M., *Our Landed Heritage: The Public Domain 1776—1936* (Princeton, 1942).

Robbins, W. G., 'Opportunity and Persistence in the Pacific Northwest. A Quantitative Study of Early Roseburg, Oregon', *Pacific Historical Review*, XXXIX (1970).

Rockoff, H., *The Free Banking Era. A Re-Examination* (New York, 1975).

Rogin, L., *The Introduction of Farm Machinery in its Relationship to the Productivity of Labour in the Agriculture of the United States during the Nineteenth Century* (Berkley, 1931).

Rohrbough, M. J., *The Trans-Appalachian Frontier. People, Societies and Institutions, 1775—1850* (New York, 1978).

Rothstein, M., 'The American Farmer and Foreign Markets, 1850—1890', in Ellis, D. M. (ed.), *The Frontier in American Development* (Ithaca, New York, 1969).

Runblom, H. and Norman, H. (eds), *From Sweden to America. A History of the Migration* (Uppsala, 1976).

Savage, W. S., *Blacks in the West* (Westport, Conn., 1976).

Schafer, J., *A History of the Pacific Northwest* (New York, 1938).

——, *The Wisconsin Lead Region* (Madison, Wisconsin, 1932).

Scheiber, H. N., *Ohio Canal Era: A Case Study of the Government and the Economy, 1820—1861* (Athens, Ohio, 1969, a).

——, 'Turner's Legacy and the Search for a Reorientation of Western History. A Review Essay', *New Mexico Historical Review*, XLIV (1969, b).

Schnell, J. C. and McLear, P. E., 'Why the Cities Grew: An Historiographical Essay on Western Urban Growth, 1850–1880', *Bulletin of the Missouri Historical Society*, XXVII (1972).

Schob, D. E., *Hired Hands and Plowboys. Farm Labour in the Midwest, 1815–60* (Urbana, Illinois, 1975).

Scott, R. V., *The Reluctant Farmer. The Rise of Agricultural Extension to 1914* (Urbana, Illinois, 1970).

Semmingsen, I., (Haugen, E. trans.), *Norway to America. A History of the Migration* (Minneapolis, 1978).

Shade, W. G., *Banks or No Banks. The Money Issue in Western Politics, 1832–65* (Detroit, 1972).

Shannon, F. A., *The Farmer's Last Frontier: Agriculture 1860–1897* (New York, 1945).

Shaw, R. E., *Erie Water West: A History of the Erie Canal, 1792–1854* (Lexington, Kentucky, 1966).

Smith, A. E., *The History of Wisconsin.* (vol. 1) *From Exploration to Statehood* (Madison, Wisconsin, 1973).

Smith, D. A., *Rocky Mountain Mining Camps. The Urban Frontier* (Bloomington, Indiana, 1967).

Smith, D. C., 'The Logging Frontier', *Journal of Forest History*, XVIII (1974).

Soltow, L., 'Inequality Amidst Abundance: Land Ownership in Early Nineteenth Century Ohio', *Ohio History*, LXXXVIII (1979).

Spence, C. C., *British Investments and the American Mining Frontier, 1860–1901* (Ithaca, New York, 1958).

Stephenson, C., 'Tracing Those Who Left: Mobility Studies and the Soundex Indexes to the United States Census', *Journal of Urban History*, 1 (1974).

Still, B., 'Patterns of Mid-Nineteenth Century Urbanization in the Middle West', *MVHR*, XXVIII (1941).

Stover, J. F., *Iron Road to the West. American Railroads in the 1850's* (New York, 1978).

Sunder, J. E., *The Fur Trade on the Upper Missouri, 1840–1865* (Norman, Oklahoma, 1965).

Swierenga, R. P., *Pioneers and Profits: Land Speculation on the Iowa Frontier* (Ames, Iowa, 1968).

——, 'Land Speculation and its Impact on American Economic Growth and Welfare. A Historiographical Review', *WHQ*, VII (1977).

Sylla, R., 'Federal Policy, Banking Market Structure and Capital Mobilization in the United States, 1863–1913', *JEH*, XXIX (1969).

Taylor G. R., *The Transportation Revolution, 1815–1860* (New York, 1951).

Taylor, P. A. M., *The Distant Magnet* (New York, 1971).

Temin, P., *The Jacksonian Economy* (New York, 1969).

Thernstrom, S., and Knights, P. R., 'Men in Motion: Some Data and Speculations about Urban Population Mobility in Nineteenth Century America', *Journal of Interdisciplinary History*, I (1970).

Thomas, B., *Migration and Economic Growth. A Study of Great Britain and the Atlantic Economy*, 2nd ed. (Cambridge, 1973).

Thornthwaite, C. W., *Internal Migration in the United States* (Philadelphia, 1934).

Throne, M., 'A Population Study of an Iowa County in 1850', *Iowa Journal of History*, LVII (1959).

——, 'Southern Iowa Agriculture, 1833–1890. The Progress from Subsistence to Commercial Corn Belt Farming', *AH*, XXIII (1949).

Tryon, R. M., *Household Manufactures in the United States 1640–1860. A Study in Industrial History* (Chicago, 1917).

Turner, F. J., 'The Significance of the Frontier in American History', *Annual Report* of the American Historical Association for 1893 (Washington, DC, 1894) reprinted in Turner F. J., *The Frontier in American History* (New York, 1920).

Udall, S. L., *The Quiet Crisis* (New York, 1963).

Unruh, J. D. Jr, *The Plains Across. The Overland Emigrants and the Trans Mississippi West, 1840–1860* (Urbana, Illinois, 1979).

Vance, J. E. Jr, *The Merchant's World. The Geography of Wholesaling* (Englewood Cliffs, New Jersey, 1970).

Van Wagenen, J. Jr, *The Golden Age of Homespun* (Ithaca, New York, 1953).

Van Zandt, F. K., *Boundaries of the United States and the Several States*, US Geol. Surv. Bull. 1212 (Washington, DC, 1966).

Vedder, R. K. and Galloway, L. E., 'Migration and the Old Northwest' in Klingaman, D. C. and Vedder, R. K. (eds), *Essays in Nineteenth Century Economic History* (Athens, Ohio, 1975).

Vinovskis, M. A., 'Socioeconomic Determinants of Interstate Fertility Differentials in the United States, in 1850 and 1860', *Journal of Interdisciplinary History*, VI (1976).

Von Nardroff, E., 'The American Frontier as a Safety-Valve – The Life, Death, Reincarnation and Justification of a Theory', *AH*, XXXVI (1962).

Wade, R. C., *The Urban Frontier. The Rise of Western Cities, 1790–1830* (Cambridge, Mass., 1959, a).

——, 'Urban Life in Western America, 1790–1830', in Scheiber, H. N. (ed.), *The Old Northwest* (Lincoln, Nebraska, 1969).

Walsh, M., *The Manufacturing Frontier. Pioneer Industry in Antebellum Wisconsin, 1830–1860* (Madison, Wisconsin, 1972).

——, 'The Dynamics of Industrial Growth in the Old Northwest, 1830–1870: An Interdisciplinary Approach', in *Business and Economic History: Papers of the Business History Conference*, 2nd ser., IV (1975).

——, 'The Spatial Evolution of the Midwestern Pork Industry, 1835–1875', *Journal of Historical Geography*, IV (1978).

Washburn, W. E., *The Indian in America* (New York, 1975).

Webb, W. P., *The Great Plains* (Boston, 1931).

Weber, D. J. (ed.), *Foreigners in Their Lands. Historical Roots of the Mexican Americans* (Albuquerque, New Mexico, 1973).

Williams, W. A., *The Roots of Modern Empire. A Study of the Growth and Shaping of Social Consciousness in a Marketplace Society* (New York, 1969).

Williamson, J. R., *Late Nineteenth Century American Development. A General Equilibrium History* (London, 1974).

Wishart, D. J., *The Fur Trade of the American West* (London, 1979).

——, 'Age and Sex Composition of the Population on the Nebraska Frontier, 1860–1880', *Nebraska History*, LIV (1973).

Wittke, C., *We Who Built America. The Saga of the Immigrant* (New York, 1940).

Young, M. E., 'Congress Looks West. Liberal Ideology and Public Land Policy in the Nineteenth Century', in Ellis, D. M. (ed.), *The Frontier in American Development* (Ithaca, New York, 1969).

Index

Pittsburgh   47, 51
Plains, *see* Northern Plains
plantations   38
Poles   69
population: density   19,   57,   60;
   family   64–5;   frontier   55–70;
   origins   67–70;   structure   60,
   63–4; western, *see* tables III, IV and
   V
prairies, *see* Midwestern farming
public domain   13, 16, 21, 22–3, 26,
   28, 29

quantification   17, 19, 25, 26, 30, 44,
   52–3, 55, 56, 65, 66, 69

railroads   37, 38, 39, 40, 41, 42, 51,
   54, 66
revisionism, *see* historians, revisionist
rivers   38, 39; *see also* under names of
   rivers
roads   35,   37;   *see   also*   wagon
   freighting
Rocky Mountains   33, 44, 48
Roseburg   65

Sacramento River   51
'safety valve'   14, 17, 67
St Louis   46, 51
San Francisco   51
Santa Fe trade   46–7
Scandinavians   69
self sufficiency   31, 32, 35, 38, 39, 41,
   53

slavery   38, 68, 69
social science   13, 14, 19, 55, 56, 66
spearheads   44, 49, 50, 65; *see* fur
   trade, lumbering *and* mining
speculation   16, 29–30, 51, 66
squatting   16, 27
stages of growth, *see* growth
steamboats   18

technology   18, 32, 33, 35, 36, 37,
   40, 41, 48, 49, 54; *see also* farm
   machinery
Teutonic germ theory   13, 14
Texas   40
'time-space matrix'   18, 32, 33, 42
towns, *see* urban growth
transport   '18, 27, 32, 33, 35, 36, 37,
   38, 39, 40, 41, 48, 49, 51, 54; *see also*
   railroads, rivers *and* roads
Turner, F. J.   11–20, 25, 31, 32, 33,
   35, 36, 37, 40, 42, 44, 46, 49, 50, 51,
   52, 54, 60, 64, 65, 66, 67, 68, 71, 72

urban growth   46, 48, 49, 50–1; and
   mobility   65, 66; and population
   63, 67
Utah   39–40, 51

wagon-freighting   38, 39, 46, 47,
   53
Wisconsin   36, 49, 51, 57
women   63, 64 *and* table V

Date Due